KT-593-496

Contents

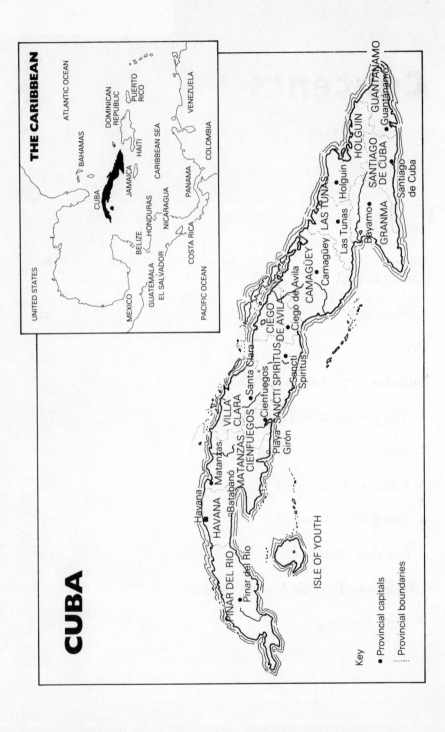

CUBA

THE CARIBBEAN

UNITED STATES

ATLANTIC OCEAN

BAHAMAS

CUBA

MEXICO

BELIZE

GUATEMALA
EL SALVADOR

HONDURAS

JAMAICA

HAITI

DOMINICAN
REPUBLIC

PUERTO
RICO

VENEZUELA

COLOMBIA

CARIBBEAN SEA

NICARAGUA

COSTA RICA

PANAMA

PACIFIC OCEAN

PINAR DEL RIO

Pinar del Río

Havana

HAVANA

Batabanó

Matanzas

MATANZAS

VILLA
CLARA

CIENFUEGOS

Cienfuegos

Santa Clara

SANCTI SPIRITUS

Sancti
Spíritus

CIEGO
DE AVILA

Ciego de Ávila

Playa
Girón

ISLE OF YOUTH

CAMAGÜEY

Camagüey

LAS TUNAS

Las Tunas

HOLGUIN

Holguín

Bayamo

GRANMA

SANTIAGO
DE CUBA

Santiago
de Cuba

GUANTANAMO

Guantánamo

Key

• Provincial capitals

····· Provincial boundaries

CUBA
THE TEST OF TIME

by
Jean Stubbs

2

First published in Great Britain in 1989 by Latin America Bureau (Research and Action) Limited, 1 Amwell Street, London EC1R 1UL

Copyright © Latin America Bureau (Research and Action) Limited 1989

British Library Cataloguing in Publication Data
Stubbs, Jean
   Cuba: the test of time
   1. Cuba, 1959-
   I. Title II. Latin America Bureau
   972.91'064

ISBN 0 906156 43 2
ISBN 0 906156 42 4 Pbk

Written by Jean Stubbs
Edited by James Ferguson
Chronology by Sarah Ross

Cover photograph by Barry Lewis/Network
Cover design by Robert Williamson
Cartoons by Nuez
Typeset, printed and bound by Russell Press, Nottingham NG7 4ET
Trade distribution in UK by Third World Publications, 151 Stratford Road, Birmingham B11 1RD
Distribution in USA by Monthly Review Press, 122 West 27th Street, New York, NY 10001

Cuba in Brief

Country and People

Area		110,860 sq km
Population (1988)	Total	10,384,600
	Growth	1.32% (1975-85)
	Urban	73%
	Rural	27%
Principal cities (1986)	Havana	2,036,800
	Santiago de Cuba	364,600

The People (1981)   According to the 1981 Census, 66% of the population was defined as 'white', 22% as 'mixed', and 12% as 'black'

Religion   Official atheism. Major churches include Roman Catholic and various Protestant denominations (Methodist, Baptist, Seventh Day Adventist, etc.) Also numerous Afro-Cuban syncretic religions

Language   Spanish

Health	1988 figures	1958 figures
Life expectancy	74	57
Infant mortality (per thousand live births)	13.3	60
Population per doctor	400	5,000
Hospital beds	65,824	25,905

Education		
Literacy	98%	76%
Primary school enrolment (%)	100%	56%

The Economy

Gross Social Product (GSP)*	1986	27,388 million pesos**
	1987	26,424 million pesos
Growth	1981-85	7.3%
	1986	1.4%
	1987	-3.2%
	1988 (1st quarter)	8.6%
Labour Force by Gender (1988)	Male	61.7%
	Female	38.3%
Labour Force by Sector (1986)	Industry	22.2%
	Agriculture/ Fishing	17.6%
	Education	11.7%
	Commerce	11.4%
	Construction	9.9%
	Health/Social Services	6.5%
	Transport	6.0%
	Other	14.6%
Unemployment (1981)		3.4%
State Budget (1987)	Total expenditure	11,798 million pesos
	Productive sector	4,456 million pesos
	Housing and community services	745 million pesos
	Education/ health	2,709 million pesos
	Social/cultural/ scientific activity	1,857 million pesos

	People's Power/other administration	565 million pesos
	Defence/public order	1,242 million pesos
	Other activities	224 million pesos

Average monthly salary (pesos) — *190/210*

Cost of living (average price in pesos)	Rent	10% maximum of income
	Bus fare	0.10 peso
	Bread (kg)	0.33 peso
	Milk (litre ration)	0.25 pesos
	Milk (litre parallel market)	1.00 peso
	Chicken (kg ration)	1.54 pesos
	Chicken (kg parallel market)	8.80 pesos
	Shoes (ration)	3-10 pesos
	Shoes (parallel market/imported)	35-100 pesos
	Refrigerator (work-place distribution)	150-200 pesos
	Refrigerator (parallel market)	1,000-1,500 pesos

Trade

Exports (socialist countries)	1986	4,699 million pesos
	1987	4,797 million pesos

Exports (market-economy countries)	1986	626 million pesos
	1987	603 million pesos

Imports (socialist countries)	1986	6,412 million pesos
	1987	6,692 million pesos

Imports (market-economy countries)	1986	1,157 million pesos
	1987	919 million pesos
Trading Partners	Exports to:	USSR 71.5%; GDR 5.22% Bulgaria 3.1%
	Imports from:	USSR 72%; GDR 4.5%; Spain 2.1%
Balance of Trade	1986	-2,244 million pesos
	1987	-2,210 million pesos
Foreign Debt (to West)	1986	US$4,985 million
	1987	US$5,657 million
	1988	US$6,260 million

*Gross Social Product 'represents the value of all productive goods and services created in the economy', but omits certain economic activities such as tourism that are deemed unproductive.

**The official exchange rate in November 1988 was US$1=0.9 peso. There exists an informal exchange rate.

Sources: Banco Nacional de Cuba, Comité Estatal de Estadísticas, *Cuba Business* (UK)

List of Abbreviations

AC	Asociación Campesina Peasant Association
ANAP	Asociación Nacional de Agricultores Pequeños National Association of Small Farmers
ANC	African National Congress
ATC	American Tobacco Company
CAP	Common Agricultural Policy (of EEC)
CCS	Cooperativa de Crédito y Servicio Credit and Service Cooperative
CDR	Comité de Defensa de la Revolución Committee for the Defence of the Revolution
CIA	Central Intelligence Agency (US)
COMECON (CMEA)	Council for Mutual Economic Assistance
CPA	Cooperativa de Producción Agropecuaria Agricultural Production Cooperative
CTC	Central de Trabajadores de Cuba Central Organisation of Cuban Trade Unions
ECLA	Economic Commission for Latin America
EEC	European Economic Community
FMC	Federación de Mujeres Cubanas Federation of Cuban Women

FMLN   Frente Farabundo Martí de Liberación Nacional
      Farabundo Marti National Liberation Front (El
      Salvador)

GLACSEC Group of Latin American and Caribbean Sugar
      Exporting Countries

INDER   Instituto Nacional de Deporte y Recreación
      National Institute of Sport and Recreation

JUCEPLAN Junta Central de Planificación
      Central Planning Board

NESL   North East Shipbuilders Ltd (UK)

OAS   Organisation of American States

PCC   Partido Comunista Cubano
      Cuban Communist Party

SA   Sociedad Agrícola
      Agricultural Society

SDPE   Sistema de Dirección y Planificación de la Economía
      Economic Management and Planning System

SELA   Sistema Económico Latino-Americano
      Latin American Economic System

SWAPO   South West Africa People's Organisation

UMAP   Unidad Militar de Apoyo a la Producción
      Military Unit for Production

UNCTAD   United Nations Commission on Trade and
      Development

UNDP   United Nations Development Programme

UNEAC   Unión de Escritores y Artistas de Cuba
      Union of Writers and Artists of Cuba

Chronology

1959   (Liberation Year)

January	Victory of the revolution: Fidel Castro enters Havana: revolutionary general strike
March	Agrarian reform initiated
August	USSR announces purchase of 170,000 tons of sugar from Cuba
September	Che Guevara signs treaties with several Asian and African countries
November	Che Guevara designated head of National Bank
December	Cuba obtains US$100 million credit in Europe

1960   (Agrarian Reform Year)

February	Sugar *centrales* nationalised
March	French ship carrying arms to Cuba sabotaged. At burial of victims, Castro uses slogan 'Patria o Muerte!' for first time
	Central Planning Board (JUCEPLAN) established
April	United Fruit Company *latifundios* expropriated
	Labour Census begun
May	Diplomatic relations with the USSR reestablished
June	Texaco refinery nationalised
July	Esso and Shell refineries taken over
	US cancels Cuba's sugar quota
	Decision to expropriate all US property
	China and Cuba sign mutual benefit treaties
August	Federation of Cuban Women (FMC) formed
	North Korea and Cuba establish diplomatic relations
September	Committees for the Defence of the Revolution (CDRs) set up
October	Major foreign banks nationalised
	US embargo on all imports to Cuba
	Urban Reform Law passed
December	Diplomatic relations established with Vietnam

1961   (Education Year)

January	US severs diplomatic relations with Cuba

	Czech government agrees to represent Cuba in US
	Uruguay expels Cuban ambassador
	Literacy campaign begun
April	Abortive US-backed mercenary invasion at Bay of Pigs (Playa Girón)
	Castro declares Cuba to be socialist
September	Cuba and USSR sign joint communique in Moscow
November	Venezuela severs diplomatic relations with Cuba
December	Colombia severs diplomatic relations with Cuba

1962   (Year of Planning)

January	Organisation of American States (OAS) expels Cuba
February	Argentina severs diplomatic relations with Cuba
	Adult literacy courses begun
	Polio vaccination campaign initiated
March	Food rationing begun
April	Ecuador breaks diplomatic relations with Cuba
June	Record coffee harvest
October	'Missile crisis': Kennedy demands withdrawal of Soviet troops and armaments from Cuba and imposes naval blockade. Kruschev accedes to demand on condition that Cuba receives guarantee of non-aggression from West
November	Kennedy suspends naval blockade but reiterates support for political and economic aggression against Cuba

1963   (Year of Organisation)

February	Commercial agreement between Cuba and USSR
March	Kennedy states 'We will build a wall around Cuba' in Costa Rica speech, leading to Central America declaration to isolate Cuba
July	Expropriation of US embassy property
September	Attack by US planes in Las Villas province
October	Second Agrarian Reform Law takes effect
November	Compulsory military service introduced

1964   (Year of the Economy)

January	Castro visits Moscow
February	US expels 700 Cubans working at Guantánamo military base

| August | Chile severs diplomatic ties with Cuba |

1965   **(Year of Agriculture)**

March	Cuba donates 10,000 tons of sugar to Vietnam
September	15,000 students mobilised for coffee harvest
October	Founding of restructured Cuban Communist Party (PCC)
December	Graduation of first primary school teachers

1966   **(Year of Solidarity)**

| January | Creation of Organisation for Solidarity between the Peoples of Africa, Asia and Latin America: first conference on tri-continental solidarity held in Havana |
| June | First national book fair |

1967   **(Heroic Vietnam Year)**

| October | Che Guevara dies in Bolivia |

1968   **(Year of the Heroic Guerrilla)**

| May | Cuba refuses to sign UN non-proliferation treaty 'Revolutionary Offensive' launched; 56,000 small private concerns are nationalised |

1969   **(Year of Decisive Effort)**

| January | Inauguration of Institute of Nuclear Physics |

1970   **(Year of Ten Million)**

| July | Record 8.5 million tons sugar harvest; but 1.5 million tons short of target |
| November | Chile reestablishes diplomatic links after election of Salvador Allende government |

1971   **(Productivity Year)**

February	Pioneer youth organisation founded
October	Peru invites Cuba to join Group of 77
November	Castro visits Allende's Chile

1972   (Year of Socialist Emulation)

May	Cuba reelected as member of UN Development Programme Administrative Council
July	Progressive military Velasco regime in Peru reestablishes diplomatic relations with Cuba, severed since 1960
	Cuba joins COMECON
December	Diplomatic relations established with Barbados, Guyana, Jamaica and Trinidad-Tobago

1973   (20th Anniversary Year)

March	Cuba has the lowest child mortality rate in Latin America
April	National discussion over judiciary reform
May	Cuba and Argentina agree to reestablish diplomatic relations
September	Castro goes to Algiers for conference of non-aligned countries
	Cuba severs diplomatic relations with Israel
	Freeze of all Chilean assets in country after death of Allende
October	Cuban merchant ship detained by US in Panama canal
November	13th Congress of Central Organisation of Trade Unions (CTC) links wages to productivity

1974   (15th Anniversary Year)

January	Brezhnev visits Cuba
February	Government offers more than 98,200 grants to young students
March	International Women's Day. Discussion of projected Family Code

1975   (Year of the 1st Congress)

January	Cuba and the Federal Republic of Germany reestablish diplomatic relations
February	Long-distance telephone line between Moscow and Havana finished
	Family Code approved
March	Cuba and Colombia reestablish diplomatic relations

July	Cuba establishes diplomatic links with Ethiopia
December	First Congress of the PCC: approval given to cooperative movement, People's Power and centralised planning system

1976   (Year of 20th Anniversary of *Granma*)

February	Referendum approves the new Constitution which is proclaimed on the 24th
March	Cuba and Libya establish diplomatic relations
April	Pirate launch attacks Cuban fishing vessels
	Bomb explodes in Cuban embassy in Lisbon
June	Bomb explodes in Cuban mission to the UN
October	Municipal elections for the National Assembly of People's Power

1977   (Year of Institutionalisation)

February	Costa Rica and Cuba reestablish diplomatic relations
March/April	Castro on six-week tour of African, Arab and Eastern European socialist countries
May	Decision by US and Cuba to open interest sections in each other's countries

1978   (Year of 11th Festival)

April	Cuba and USSR sign important protocol on commercial exchange
June	7.3 million tons of sugar produced
August	11th International Youth Festival held in Havana
September	Spain and Cuba sign agreement on scientific and technical collaboration
December	Exhibition 'Cuba: 20 Years of Revolution'

1979   (20th Anniversary of Victory)

April	Municipal Assembly elections; 96.9% of population votes
	Grenada and Cuba establish diplomatic relations
June	Government denounces US plans to intervene in Nicaragua
July	Nicaragua and Cuba reestablish diplomatic relations

September	6th Summit of the Non-Aligned Countries held in Havana
December	1st International Festival of New Latin American Cinema

1980   (Year of 2nd Congress)

March	Cuba signs resolution in UN against discrimination against women
April	Boatlift from port of Mariel; 125,000 Cubans leave for the US
May	Opening of Farmers' Markets
December	Second Congress of the PCC

1981   (20th Anniversary of Playa Girón)

January	Cuba and Panama issue joint communique condemning abuse of human rights in El Salvador
February	Foreign Ministry denounces South African invasion of Mozambique
August	Castro visits Mexico
	Cuba pledges renewed support to Angola against invasion by South African troops

1982   (24th Year of the Revolution)

May	Cuba condemns British action in the Falklands/Malvinas
	ANAP Congress debates Farmers' Markets
November	*Granma* publishes list of 'imperialist infamies' carried out against the Cuban regime

1983   (30th Anniversary of Moncada)

March	Agreement for refinancing of Cuba's foreign debt signed in Paris
May	US senator Barry Goldwater expresses desire to convert Cuba into the 51st State
October	US invades Grenada: 24 Cuban construction workers killed in fighting with US troops

1984 **(25th Anniversary of the Triumph of the Revolution)**

April — Election to People's Power — 98.6% of registered voters vote

June — Cuba decides not to attend Los Angeles Olympics

November — Law passed to make all tenants house-owners

December — Cuba-US talks on migratory relations. Cuba agrees to take back 2,700 criminals and 'undesirables' who went to US during the Mariel boatlift

1985 **(Year of the 3rd Congress)**

January — Intense debate on Housing Law and Labour Code

March — Gorbachev comes to power

December — Third Congress of PCC

1986 **(Year of the 30th Anniversary of the *Granma* landing)**

April — Cuba condemns US attack on Libya

May — Cuba proposes postponement of payments on debts due in 1986. Farmers' Markets closed

December — Deferred third PCC Congress session: Castro announces beginning of 'rectification' campaign

1987 **(Year 29 of the Revolution)**

February — Infant mortality down to 13.6:1000

1988 **(Year 30 of the Revolution)**

August — Castro visits Ecuador to attend inauguration of newly elected President Borja

September — UN Human Rights Commission visits Cuba. Negotiations over Angola and southern Africa with South Africa and US

December — Castro visits Mexico to attend inauguration of newly elected President Salinas

Preface

Impressions of any country or place are almost always coloured by where the traveller is coming from. Havana looks very different flying in from Paris, London or New York, than from Mexico City, Kingston or Managua. Even when there is familiarity with the terrain, perceptions change according to the point of departure.

I flew into Havana in mid-August 1988, twenty years to the night after I had first flown there, in 1968. On both occasions, I was arriving from London. Though I lived in Havana for the better part of those 20 years in between, I found I carried some of my British perceptions that I had not had on other occasions when returning there from other parts of the Caribbean or Latin America. It was not so much the potholes of underdevelopment or the lacklustre of blockade that struck me, nor even the crowded buses and the ubiquitous queues; what was uppermost was an impatience for things to function better, and the feeling that they feasibly could and should, even within some tough national and international constraints. A European response, perhaps, but it was one many on the island shared with me, from well-placed officials to friends and acquaintances and people on the street.

The year 1968 was when the effects of internal economic upheaval and external blockade threatened to outweigh the gains of the young revolution. There was little in the shops, and rationing was at its height. Yet, it was also a period of revolutionary euphoria, hardly dampened by the death of Ernesto 'Che' Guevara. The year 1988 was one of external economic crisis and internal economic difficulties. On a different plane from the 1960s, however, they came in the wake of the boom of the late 1970s and early 1980s. Again, the shops were looking barer and more goods were back on ration. Strikingly, the year was one of a return to Che and to his legacy of political and economic thought. There was also — sometimes oblique, sometimes

1

explicit — an outspokenness on problems and policies that was casting around for an outlet. The form that it takes only time will tell. But the moment is certainly one to lend itself to reflection.

Thirty years since the revolution, twenty since I first made its acquaintance, this book aims to take a critical look from within at the options and dilemmas facing a small nation which has fought against the odds, taken on one of the world's giants and traded it in for another. Yet, despite all the difficulties encountered, this people has achieved levels of development and an independence of spirit that gives Cuba a world presence incommensurate with size.

Jean Stubbs

London, January 1989

Introduction: Dollars for Gold

'Gold fever' hit Havana in 1988. In the capital city of a country that can boast no great riches but no great poverty either, this was how people were describing the rush to trade in gold and silver objects for coveted luxury consumer goods. A handful of newly opened state stores offering imported clothing and appliances were wittily dubbed 'Hernán Cortés', in a reference to one of the most infamous of the early Spanish *conquistadores* who exchanged trinkets for the gold and silver of Latin America's indigenous population.

People seemed to be ahead of the government in making some obvious connections. The gold and silver was for state export to help redress Cuba's hard currency shortage. In return, those selling were able to satisfy consumer needs not met by the domestic market. But they were also able to analyse their loss of objects of value for consumer items, to question the exchange price they were being offered and to recognise historical parallels.

Another joke among friends was the advice to avoid wearing gold or silver jewelry anyway, since it was only likely to be stolen. This popular wisdom reflected people's misgivings over the new 'decriminalisation' programme. Contrary to widely held views in the West, Cuba has a far from closed prison policy. Government commitment has been to open-plan prisons and re-education schemes, with evidence of improving conditions even in maximum security and political prisoner wings. In late 1987, there was a further relaxation of the penal code, whereby 60 different offences were to be dealt with by reduced sentences or fines. Since this measure was backdated, several thousand prisoners in jail for minor criminal offences were released on probation. In certain areas, such as Havana, they were adding to an already tense job market and were fuelling people's expectations of an increased petty crime rate.

The jokes were not well received in all quarters. The August 1988 edition of the Communist Party publication *El Militante Comunista* ran an article entitled 'Una decisión necesaria' by way of explanation of the shops. Important measures affecting the internal running of the country are often subject to considerable public scrutiny, if not prior debate. For such a potentially sensitive one, it was therefore all the more surprising that people should not have been informed. This article was seen as rather overdue, to say the least.

Basically, the argument for the controversial shops hinged on calculations to the effect that through them, in just two years, the state could obtain US$100 million. The state's need for that money stemmed from a 1987 foreign debt with Western market economies of US$5,657 million. Of this, since many of the country's Western trade and credit lines are pegged to the dollar, US$300 million was directly attributable to the fall in that currency's value.

There is no doubt but that the blockade on Cuba by its major pre-revolutionary trading partner, the US, is what has placed the greatest obstacles in the way of Cuba's development. For three decades the country's most implacable enemy has sought to isolate Cuba in the West and has certainly precipitated the island's entry into the mainstream socialist camp. By the mid-1980s, a fluctuating 15-30 per cent of trading was with Western economies, and, by 1988, was much closer to the lower figure. The economy has consequently been considerably buffered from the shockwaves of capitalist world economic trends. Even so, the country has still fallen into its own debt trap with the West. In 1986, the island experienced a 40 per cent loss in foreign earnings, due to the depressed price of sugar on the international market and also the fall in world oil prices. Cuba had been importing Soviet crude and exporting Cuban refined, edging out sugar as the country's main hard currency earner.

The only solution, it was argued, was to cut imports from the West to half the 1986 value of nearly US$1,200 million and buy only essential parts and raw materials needed for production. The year 1986 was the first that Cuba was forced to default on its Western foreign debt obligations (it first requested rescheduled payments in 1982). In 1987 it managed to renegotiate its trade debt with the Paris Group (the Paris Club of rich Western nations minus the US), and was involved in heavy renegotiating of its financial debt in 1988.

While not on a scale parallel to the rest of Latin America and the Caribbean, the debt has forced the government to step up exports, cut down imports and, where possible, push through more import substitution, as well as introduce certain austerity measures. Unlike the case in many neighbouring countries, the policy is intended to achieve immediate aims in a way that does not hold back long-term economic development programmes and spreads the burden evenly. It is to be done without hitting any sector unduly or undercutting social spending, such as health and education, where there have been very substantial advances for such a small underdeveloped country. Hence, the attempts to seek out new, as well as strengthen already established, sources of dollar income — and the shops. 'Is that option not preferable to sacrificing any of our five-year development plans?' the article asked. The state would far prefer to be able to satisfy such consumer desires on a mass scale, but is tied to apportioning out resources where they are most needed. This would continue to be the case, it was argued, until the material wealth had been created for an abundance of consumer items.

The same reasons might be given for the equally controversial 'dollar shops' and the whole dual dollar/peso economy which puts dollar-bearing foreigners and Cubans at the same distinct advantage as their gold- and silver-bearing Cuban counterparts. The dollar shops were a source of great irritation in the early 1980s, when they were used extensively by Cubans resident in the US visiting Cuba under the family reunification programme. The revolutionary principle of distribution according to merit and need was seen to be violated as US Cubans showered dollar gifts on their island relatives.

They did so as Cuba was embarking on a substantial tourist development programme. Designed as a dollar-spinning industry of Caribbean sun, sea and sand, it was also to show the visitor just what a socialist society was achieving for its people. However, the industry began to produce its own spin-off, which was the tourist hustler, avid for dollar exchange, access to dollar areas and dollar goods. Veritable tourist enclaves were not always calculated to give the more positive image Cuba had hoped for, and the hustlers' booty added to the common knowledge of enclave privilege.

The gold and silver shops therefore only served to exacerbate an already growing malaise, and one Cuba will have to contend with as long as it operates a dual distribution system and there are consumer shortages. What specially jarred, moreover, was that the new exchange shops came into their own just as the few imported consumer goods were beginning to become more scarce, as a result of the very economic crisis that occasioned the thirst for dollars. At the same time, because more goods needed to be earmarked for export and export lines were generally prioritised, and because many a domestic production line needed some crucial dollar-market input, domestic consumer shortages began to be felt. Toilet paper,

5

toothpaste, deodorant and matches were among some of the more basic items that were unavailable.

Despite efforts to the contrary, certain foodstuffs were also less easy to come by. The pressure was on prioritising cash crops for export; the weather took its toll in the form of heavy rains and flooding after prolonged drought; the other side to the coin of agricultural technification was a problem such as tractors out of action for want of spare parts; and, while production levels were kept surprisingly high in the circumstances, state mechanisms proved cumbersome and inadequate for marketing. As a result, certain items which had been plentiful enough to have been taken off rationing had to be rationed again to guarantee a minimum for all. The contrast between the dollar and the peso markets could not have been greater, and this contrast was not one to fit easily with the rhetoric of political rethinking.

Renewed Revolutionary Offensive

In 1986, President Fidel Castro had launched a new 'revolutionary offensive', appealing to socialist morality and ethics, with a retrenchment of market controls and increased centralised planning as a prerequisite for social equity. Consumerism was firmly placed as a low priority; production had to come first. Called a process of 'rectification' of errors, it has included the closing of avenues for possible individual enrichment. Reminiscent of the revolutionary offensive of the late 1960s when small businesses and shops were closed down, it targeted what were seen as hustlers of an old and new kind: from middlemen and petty street vendors doing nicely out of market liberalisation, to factory managers profiting from contractual arrangements, workers benefiting from low-pegged work norms, and bureaucrats involved in fraud, embezzlement and corruption.

Market liberalisation or the small private trading sector was most short-lived and the first to go. Private craft and farmers' markets were allowed to open at the beginning of the 1980s, but were soon closed down for lack of controls. Although controls were supposedly introduced when they subsequently reopened, the policy was deemed to have backfired half a decade later. The May 1986 decision to close the 'free' markets caused a national and international stir. And yet they accounted for less than two per cent of total market transactions. Since the land reform and nationalisation of the early 1960s and the closing down of small-time private production in the late 1960s, the state had taken over all manufacturing, trade and services, plus the major part of agriculture, and it controlled all official, if not informal

Julio Etchart

sector or black market, outlets. It had also introduced rationing as an equitable way of allocating scarcer food resources at state-subsidised prices.

In the late 1970s, parallel state markets were introduced to sell small surpluses of all kinds of products, including agricultural ones,

---

Castro Speaks

'We began to go off course...with the blind belief that the construction of socialism is basically a question of mechanisms... We've harboured two kinds of illusion. When the Constitution was enacted, the country's political-administrative division was carried out and the People's Power organs were set up...the naive belief came about that the state was going to function perfectly, almost automatically. Later we started to realise that this called for important political work by the Party... In the sphere of material production and the services...we started believing everything would run perfectly with the economic management and planning system...a panacea that would almost build socialism by itself...many of our comrades dressed up as capitalists, started acting like capitalists, but without the capitalists' efficiency... Capitalists who manage to survive competition are demanding, very demanding, or else they don't survive. Where there's no competition, if the motivation prompting the owner in a capitalist society to defend his personal interests is out of the question, what is there to substitute? Only the cadres' individual sense of responsibility, the role played by cadres... We have achieved success in other activities thanks to good political work in health, education, defence... A consciousness, a communist spirit, a revolutionary will and vocation, were, are and will always be a thousand times more powerful than money.'
Speech to the deferred Party Congress session, 2 December 1986.

'Rectification is not idealism, but realism, better use of the economic management and planning system which right now is like a lame nag with two-bit capitalist hucksters. What are we rectifying? We're rectifying all those things — and there are many — that strayed from the revolutionary spirit, from revolutionary work, revolutionary virtue, revolutionary effort, revolutionary responsibility; all those things that strayed from the spirit of solidarity among people. We're rectifiying all the shoddiness and mediocrity that is precisely the negation of Che's ideas, his revolutionary thought, his style, his spirit and his example.'
Speech to mark 20 years since Che Guevara's death, 8 October 1987

'This revolution has been characterised by a creativity and reluctance to copy from others. If we'd followed the stereotypes, no revolution

---

at slightly higher prices. Individual farmers were encouraged to form cooperatives to boost private sector agricultural production. Private farmers' markets, it was hoped, would also help to stimulate production in sensitive areas that the state had failed to cater to, such as fresh fruit and vegetables for domestic consumption. As a result

would have been made here...yet we created the subjective conditions... Our agrarian reform did not divide up land... We developed the principle of combining study and work...powerful mass organisations... I've had occasion to criticise our fervour in applying our own interpretations and neglecting positive experiences of the socialist countries; but we've also copied negative experiences of the socialist countries. Now we'll go on searching for our own paths, our own formulas.'
Speech to mark 35 years since the Moncada attack, 26 July 1987.

'It's not hard to defend socialism when times are easy and it's in fashion... It is hard in the face of international and national difficulties, some due to our own errors and some beyond our control.

Our error is not having done more and better over 30 years; in making mistakes, some of which stem from imitating the experiences of other socialist countries, many of which they're now saying are no use. We don't want them to be telling us in ten or 20 years time that what they're doing now is no use. That's why we should base ourselves on our own experiences, ideas, and interpretations...

But we should not be discouraged by these difficulties, nor those stemming from objective conditions in the world today, in which thousands of millions of people are plundered by neo-colonialist, imperialist powers... on the contrary, we should raise our voice in common struggle... We should be prepared to face all difficulties and all aggression, to fight on every terrain...

Reforms are taking place in the socialist camp, especially the USSR. If they're successful, it will be good for socialism and for us all. If they run into serious difficulties, the consequences will be hard, especially for us. We can expect difficulties from the enemy camp and difficulties that might come from our own friends. But not even that should discourage us.

We're a fighting people, setbacks have not got the better of us, and we've come through difficult times. We won when we were just a handful. Today we're millions, and no external or internal force, no objective or subjective conditions can hold back our victorious march to the future.'
Speech on Armed Forces Day, 5 December 1988.

of the markets, supplies of vegetables, fruit, meat and poultry were more readily available. However, farmers, middlemen and truckers all eventually came under attack, for exorbitant pricing and considerable syphoning-off of state resources to private sector dealings for personal gain. There was already talk in government circles of closing the markets down when a cooperative farmers' meeting was so outspoken about the individual private farming sector's abuse of the market that an overnight decision was taken.

Since then, a determined state and cooperative effort has been made for production levels to be maintained and for produce to go through the state rationing and state parallel marketing systems. However, in the absence of efficient distribution, freezing and canning, market shortages still alternate with seasonal gluts. What is especially irksome for the consumer is the lengthy, unwieldy nature of selling procedures, causing unnecessarily long queues. Yet, unless there is a major shift in policy, a return to market liberalisation appears unlikely.

The demise of the 'free farmers' market', as it was known, signalled the end of other peripheral internal market situations deriving from the free flow of contractual arangements. A garlic farmer might have made 50,000 pesos a year by privately selling his surplus after meeting state quotas. Similarly, an artist was reported to have earned 180,000 pesos by selling his paintings to state institutions. Neither was doing anything illegal, but each was making much more than the average yearly wage of only 2,000 pesos, or 5,000 a year for a doctor. Others were doing nicely from measures introduced to help ease the housing problem. The state had engaged in major housing construction programmes and had begun to authorise some private home building and repair work. In 1985 it was decided to give all state housing tenants the right to buy their previously state-controlled homes; a home for everyone had been one of the tenets of Fidel Castro's 1953 Moncada Programme that had been a blueprint for the revolution, and it was felt that people both had a right to buy and would take more pride in a home of their own. The buying and selling of property was also permitted on the residual private housing market. Property prices, especially in Havana, boomed in less than six months and the new law was repealed. The right to buy from the state is still guaranteed by law, but private buying and selling have been stopped, at least until prices can be controlled, probably through the state as an intermediary.

By mid-1986, certain key parts of the state sector were coming in for criticism. This criticism extended even to the celebrated post-revolutionary health programme which has been rightly praised, especially in the context of a country that cannot guarantee enormous resources to pay for it. Health has been a major priority of the revolution, so complaints in the mid-1980s about Havana hospitals were all the more cause for concern. Major hospital construction programmes had been held up through poor planning and chaotic decentralisation of construction enterprises, and there was an impressive list of unfinished projects. This was an observable trend for other branches of the economy and also tied in with low-set production targets and bloated payrolls, making for low productivity and low profitability.

The many lengthy speeches and interventions of President Castro on the subject, and what might otherwise have been more or less secret deliberations were given extensive live television coverage. This included three- and five-day meetings of cooperative farmers, managers, party and union representatives of state industrial and agricultural enterprises on a province by province basis, analysing in detail the nature of problems that had arisen and possible solutions. The emphasis was laid on there being no fast or easy measures, underlining that remedies had to be sought in each particular case. They ranged from more realistic production targets and better organisation of the shopfloor to innovative methods of import substitution, and the like.

The official battle against economic inefficiency has veered away from market pulls and what is seen as economicism (or policy-making based exclusively on economic criteria) to a campaign for more efficient central planning and coordination and greater worker consciousness. A return to voluntary work and the values of disinterested labour was envisaged. A major example of this has been the revived microbrigade movement in housing and other construction, calling into play more moral as well as material incentives. Microbrigades were introduced in the 1970s as a way of pushing through housing construction when there were labour shortages, especially in the construction sector. In effect, people were seconded from their regular jobs for a given period of time, usually anywhere from six months to six years, and those left behind were to double up on their work. The allocation of housing was then tied to the workplace and the effort put in by workers in the microbrigades and their colleagues at the office or factory.

The microbrigades were gradually phased out in the early 1980s, among other things because they were considered uneconomic and the finished housing was judged substandard. No other programme replaced them. The result was that state housing figures fell to the same level as private home building, largely in rural areas. In the

11

Julio Etchart

Microbrigade in action, Havana

cities especially, housing needs went unmet. There was no longer an overall shortage of labour, but there were problems in attracting labour into certain sectors, such as construction.

Thanks to the state education programme of the last three decades, Cuba's is an educated population, and the attraction is, on the whole, to more skilled and professional jobs. At the same time, there is overmanning in many areas that range from heavy industry to government offices. The revived microbrigade movement could help meet a social and economic need in housing and other construction by reallocating human resources from one sector to another, without creating unemployment and discontent. It was also hoped to imbue in people a renewed sense of commitment and purpose to a collective goal. The major drawback to buildings being so rapidly constructed with semi-skilled labour continues to be one of standards, and there have been instances of brand-new nurseries that have had to close down temporarily because of leaking. There has at least been an attempt to improve architectural design and to stop building the more problematical high-rise apartment blocks.

The striving for better quality was accompanied by an emphasis on moral commitment. Reward was very much tied in with the community benefiting from such amenities, and not simply with money and entrepreneurship. The fact that this came just as other socialist countries were easing restraints on entrepreneurship has been seen as a return to the spirit of the 1960s, when revolutionaries like Ernesto 'Che' Guevara, rather than hard-headed economists, formulated policy. It was the Argentinian-born Che who spearheaded the debate over moral and material incentives, the notion of the 'New Man', and a more questioning approach to drawing up a socialist model for a small underdeveloped Caribbean island state.

The questioning has in a sense come full circle in the 1980s, but, it is argued in Cuba, this is a qualitatively new phase in a well established debate. In 1987, it was the 20th anniversary of Che's assassination in Bolivia; in 1988, the 60th anniversary of Che's birth. Each was an occasion to evoke the debates of the time about revolutionary ideas and values. It should be said that Che's presence has always been intensely felt in Cuba. Billboards and offices are filled with his image. The Pioneer Organisation of primary and secondary school children has the motto 'We'll grow up like Che'. And the introduction of a more Soviet-type economic management and planning system in the mid-1970s was painstakingly presented as no real departure from Che's thinking, just as much as today's changes are legitimised in these terms.

13

The state versus market and moral versus material incentive debate is perhaps one that is destined to be fought out for a long time in socialist thinking and practice. While it may be argued that, in the simplest terms of Marxist philosophy, ideas and feelings are primarily determined by material and economic reality and not vice-versa, in contemporary Cuba, there are some hard economic reasons for emphasising the moral dimension of work incentives.

Austerity measures were first announced in December 1986, when cutbacks were brought before the National Assembly of People's Power. They included some minor reductions in rationed foodstuffs and consumer goods, and energy-saving reductions in all branches of the economy. This ranged from major economising on fuel in industry to reduced media transmission time and a doubling of city bus fares from a flat rate of five cents to ten. The increased fares were intended to take the strain off the buses (and thereby give people more exercise to help offset a growing problem of sedentary lifestyles and obesity) by actively discouraging short-distance bus trips. In the heat of the summer of 1988, city people, especially in Havana, may have ended up walking — not out of choice but because a shortage of spare parts had drastically reduced the number of buses on the road.

The New Man

'The danger lies in not seeing the wood for the trees. The illusion of building socialism on the legacy of well-worn weapons of capitalism (commodity, profitability, individual material interest as the lever, etc) can be a dead-end alley. After travelling a long distance, paths may have often crossed and it may be difficult to see where a wrong road was taken. Meanwhile, the adapted economic base has undermined the development of consciousness. To build communism, along with the material base there has to be a new man in the making.

That is why it is so important to choose the right tool for mobilising the masses. That tool has to be basically moral, without obviating a correct use of material incentive, especially of a social kind.

In moments of extreme danger it is easy to invoke moral incentives; for them to remain relevant, there needs to be developed an awareness that has the values of a new category. Society as a whole must become one huge school.'

Che Guevara (Reprinted in the ANAP magazine, March 1988)

A Country in Hock

Cuba is seen in the West as a country in hock to the USSR, since hidden subsidies exist in its trading relations with that country in particular. Cuba sees this more in terms of fair prices on a sliding scale operated by the socialist camp's COMECON, in which Cuba, along with Mongolia and Vietnam, enjoys favoured nation status. In one sense, this arrangement is not very different from the favoured trading status accorded by Britain to Commonwealth countries, just as, even taking the highest figures quoted for Soviet subsidies, they are hardly any different from those the US pumps into its nearby Commonwealth State of Puerto Rico. And when it comes to sugar, Cuba's main product, few countries market the bulk of their sugar at going world market prices. To some extent, then, COMECON represents for Cuba what might be seen as the beginnings of a new international economic order.

And yet, the course charted is by no means an even one. It is no secret that the USSR, and socialist trading partners in general, are demanding greater economic efficiency of Cuba. In the summer of 1987, some Soviet economists were arguing that *perestroika* or the restructuring of economic and political practices had to be applied to international trading relations within the socialist camp. At COMECON meetings since, Cuba would seem to have defended its position. So far, there has been no qualitative change in the nature of relations between the less developed and more developed COMECON partners.

There are grounds for thinking that Moscow cannot be particularly enthusiastic about Cuba's rectification process. Conversely, there have been some strong, if usually veiled, indications that Havana is not overjoyed with *perestroika*. Rectification is quite similar to *perestroika* in that its objectives — greater economic efficiency and the removal of possible avenues for corruption — are the same. Rectification has not, however, looked to the introduction of market mechanisms as a vehicle for reform, but to their abolition.

For the early part of 1988 there was tacit mutual recognition of the particularity of the different socialisms, arising out of different cultures and traditions and situations, each with its own levels of development and developmental needs. Soviet restructuring stems from the dictates of Soviet realities, Cuba maintained. Cuban rectification is rooted in Cuban reality. It would be wrong to try to apply the one to the other; in President Castro's words, this would amount to treating a headache with a corn-plaster. Towards the end of the year, however, official pronouncements became progressively

15

more loaded, implying that some of the island's problems stemmed from imitating certain Soviet experiences, which Soviet reforms were in fact aimed at, but in a very different direction. Cuba suggested that it had come through the experiment of market liberalisation and had first-hand knowledge of the problems that it had generated.

The leadership might have been irritated by the contrasts drawn between the two countries' approaches to economic reform, but again the Cuban *vox populi* coined its jocular terms for the moment: 'perestropica' and 'Castroika'. That the Spanish-language edition of *Moscow News*, with its new-found controversial coverage of internal Soviet events, had in two years jumped from being one of the least to one of the most popular weekly magazines suggested that the Cuban public was eager to learn what was going on in the sister socialist country and to draw its own conclusions.

Rectification soon became a catch-all word, which was on the lips of all Cubans but which nobody could clearly define. Most generally taken to mean the rectification of errors in the economic field, it also took in the political and socio-cultural, including informatics. In a sense, therefore, it covered what in the USSR would be *perestroika*, or economic restructuring, and *glasnost* (transparency or ideological openness). In the USSR, it was held that there could not be one without the other: *perestroika* and *glasnost* were a complementary liberalising of the economy and society. In Cuba, on the other hand, rectification was seen as a tightening up of the economy with a potentially paradoxical liberalisation of society.

The way in which the paradox has been played out has to be viewed in the context of three external forces: the somewhat ambiguous pressures, but ultimately overwhelming support, from the socialist countries; positive developments towards unity with Latin America and the Third World on a range of issues; and the negative impact of continued political hostility from the West, particularly from Cuba's nearby and relentless enemy, the US.

One recent turn of events took much of Cuba by surprise. In late 1987, the US named a new chief of its Interests Section in Havana. One of the State Department's Far East experts, he appeared to be the highest-ranking official to have been sent to Cuba since the Interests Section was opened. His brief was clearly to improve relations with Cuba, and one outcome in December 1987 was the revived 1984 Cuba-US Migratory Agreement that had been suspended by Cuba in 1985. The Migratory Agreement had come as a welcome point of family reunification, enabling family visits between the two countries, when possibly one in three Cuban families has relatives in the US. Cuba's suspension of the agreement had been triggered by the US-sponsored establishment of a radio station that bore the name of the 19th-century Cuban independence hero, José Martí. The station was not substantially different from the usual Voice of America in terms of its anti-communist propaganda, but was seen as deliberately adding insult to injury by its choice of name.

The renewal of the Migratory Agreement appeared curious under the Reagan administration, which went out of its way to be unaccommodating to Cuba. Both 1987 and 1988 saw Washington try, but fail, to pass a motion through the UN's Geneva Commission on Human Rights, censuring Cuba for human rights violations. The human rights issue is part of a whole US disinformation campaign against Cuba on various fronts, which involves some not so behind-the-scenes political pressure being brought to bear, especially on smaller, more vulnerable countries for their vote against Cuba in international forums. There is an argument to be made that what is on the agenda is less the issue of human rights than an obvious political animosity. The US record on certain human rights issues is none too exemplary, the Cuban government is quick to point out, and the US has been forced to tone down its allegations against Cuba. From alleged killings and torture, and ill-treatment in the prisons, the US case against Cuba now rests more on allegations of arbitrary arrest and lack of freedom of association and travel.

In 1987, an array of Cuban ex-prisoners with highly dubious past histories were paraded by the US in Geneva. In 1988, the US delegation was headed by Armando Valladares, a member of the police during the pre-revolutionary dictatorship of Fulgencio Batista. Valladares was jailed in 1961 on charges of sabotage, but claimed to be a poet-prisoner of conscience. Allegedly an invalid in a wheelchair and the object of an international campaign, Valladares surprised the world by walking off a *Cubana* plane upon landing in Paris. In the meantime, Cuba has released the great majority of its long-time political prisoners and opened its prisons for visiting US and other delegations to inspect. The 1988 Amnesty International report went some way to dispelling the image of the 'tropical gulag', and the UN Commission of Inquiry report is likely to follow suit. The Cuban government has also allowed *ad hoc* human rights groups to function on the island. Small and disorganised, these groups are now campaigning for an internal political opening more than anything else.

Similarly, something of a war of the intelligence agencies came to a head. Two major defections from Cuba in the mid-1980s, Brigadier General Rafael del Pino and Cuba's intelligence person in Czechoslovakia, Florentino Azpillaga, blew the cover of an as yet unknown number of Cuban agents and double agents. The two defections caused Cuba to turn public some of its double agents, leading to charges against over 100 CIA agents in Cuba in diplomatic or tourist guise. Londoners will remember that it was Azpillaga, in an allegedly joint US and British intelligence operation, who was at the centre of a St John's Wood shooting incident in September 1988. This led to the expulsion from Britain of Cuba's commercial attache Carlos Medina Pérez and the Cuban ambassador Oscar Fernández Mell.

Cuba's often observed 'siege mentality' stems from obvious insecurities and imponderables in undertaking a sweeping revolution that has always been far from popular with a powerful enemy neighbour, though popular at home. Even so, it has only been a relatively closed mentality. Many in Cuba are quick to point out that the country has never been as closed as the USSR — a small island economy cannot afford to be. In fact, there are areas where it is felt the USSR might learn from Cuba in this respect. Cuba had never had an equivalent of Stalinism and, it could be argued, has always had a more open ideological stance.

Since the mid-1970s there has been an attempted institutionalisation of the revolution, with a certain separation of party and government, based on an electoral system for local, regional and national assemblies of *Poder Popular* (People's Power). Candidates are put up from the local constituency, voting is by secret ballot and the electorate ultimately has the power of recall over its elected representatives. Cuba is undeniably a one-party state, but within the system there are channels for non-party participation. This participatory mechanism functions better at the community level and less well when it comes to national decision-making levels. Yet this is probably true for any non-ruling party opposition in most countries, Western democracies included. The fact that Cuba has had such an immensely charismatic and popular leader as Fidel Castro makes it all the more difficult to challenge his ideas and positions within the party and state structures, the present time being no exception. The leadership question, however, is arguably one that no revolution has been able to really resolve.

Latin/Caribbean Idiosyncracy

No doubt Cuba's relative openness can be attributed in part to different geopolitical circumstances and is, perhaps, partly a question of Latin/Caribbean idiosyncracy. Revolutionary Cuba is known to have often been ready to recognise mistakes and to try to redress them. The island is also known to display a certain liveliness of debate, a theoretical *salsa*, so to speak, that is on a par with its music and dance.

Culturally, revolutionary Cuba had its most dogmatic phase in the late 1960s and early 1970s. This began to ease up after the creation of the Ministry of Culture in 1975, with Armando Hart as minister. An unspoken blacklisting of certain authors was dropped, and publications began to open up to more controversial figures and writing. Even if the film industry, which has over the years produced some excellent work on contemporary Cuba, has paradoxically not proved itself too adventurous in recent productions, film policy has always been markedly open, and Havana is now each year a venue for world filmmakers of many persuasions in the form of the New Latin American Film Festival. Like many international events hosted by Cuba, in cultural, trade, health and other fields, this has provided an open door, and acts in itself as a liberalising influence.

Among the more outspoken cultural media has been theatre, representing the symptoms of a theatrical revival after over a decade of decline. A recent series of plays has tackled controversial social issues. *Weekend in Bahía* proved to be a bold and innovative way of looking at migration to the US, split families and split personalities. Satire has also really come into its own, as in one of the more recent hits, *El Bateus de Amadeus*, based on the Milos Forman film of Salieri's rivalry with Mozart and providing a contemporary Cuban allegory of talent at odds with bureaucratic authority. There has also always been a range of experimental art work. This applies, for instance, to the magical realism of Manuel Mendive and his body painting, which takes evident strands from Afro-Cuban and Yoruba culture. A recent development has been an almost Dadaist anti-art movement, involving the deliberate distortion of political slogans, and a pop art that has a very definite anti-establishment slant.

The press has proved more resistant to the current atmosphere of criticism and experimentation. There have been some signs in certain publications, but not enough for many people's liking, even when the party itself has been calling for a more informed and more critical press since 1984. The need was perceived to be even greater in 1985 when Washington started beaming in Radio Martí, thereby intensifying media warfare and broadcasting a barrage of information, and disinformation, into Cuba. Before the year was out, there had been executive and other changes in the media. If Television Martí goes on the air in 1989, as the US intends, pressures for reform in the Cuban media will be even greater.

19

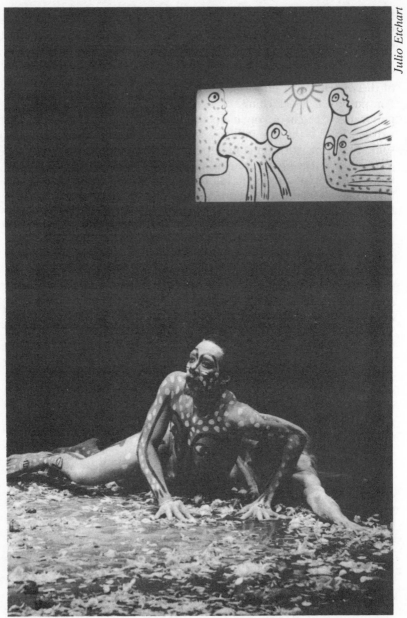

Julio Etchart

Manuel Mendive performance in London, 1988

Journalists have complained that they cannot do a better and more investigative job unless given more information and access, leading to a whole debate around the notion of self-censorship. Were the journalists afraid of going too far in exposing society's failings, or was it that doors were being closed to them when they tried to be more enterprising? The press has, however, played a role in revealing flagrant cases of inefficiency, abuse and corruption. One notorious case was that of a young woman of Jamaican descent, who worked at a cement factory in eastern Cuba and had been wrongly dismissed for criticising administrative irregularities. It was only after national attention was brought to her case by articles in the national daily *Granma* that she was reinstated.

A more recent instance of media involvement in sensitive areas occurred in June 1987 when Luis Orlando Domínguez, for many years head of the Communist Youth and at the time director of the Civil Aviation Institute, was arrested. The charges were embezzlement and corruption, and occasioned a five-hour televised explanation by President Castro himself. The unspoken question was to what extent Orlando Domínguez, was ultimately responsible for Rafael del Pino, described by Washington as 'the biggest intelligence catch we've ever had', simply piloting a plane out of Havana airport with suitcase and child the month before. By September, he had been tried and sentenced to 20 years. The 'affair' came to symbolise the rectification campaign against corruption, especially since it had been made so public. Since his was hardly believed to be a unique case, it was hoped that he was not merely a scapegoat and that other exposure cases would follow. This does not seem to have been the case, at least not frequently enough to satisfy popular demand for such revelations.

Altruism versus Pragmatism

The vulnerability of a country like Cuba is possibly what has helped fire the people's strong sense of liberation. This holds especially true where national liberation is concerned, and is the foundation for Cuba's support for other national liberation struggles, as well as its own. A current and legitimate concern among the people is what will happen in Angola after the Cuban troops withdraw and leave the Angolan people exposed to South African military aggression. Such altruism, it must be said, is also related to a more pragmatic concern as to how the domestic economy and society, with all the existing strains, can assimilate the 50,000 returnees.

21

But the liberation ethic has many dimensions: for women to achieve their emancipation within the revolution, for the black people of Cuba to reclaim their culture and beliefs (the Brown Virgin is perhaps more central to Cuba than is the Virgin Mary), and for the relatively new proponents of liberation theology. The dialogue between Church and state may be as yet less in the public eye but it is growing in significance. The debate has sprung from several sources. Within the Church itself there has been an increasing reflection, from the grass-roots upwards, on the writings of the Gospel and the ethical values of socialist revolution. This movement has been paralleled by a willingness within the party and the state to enter into dialogue with the Church. A party religious affairs office was elevated in 1985 from the Central Committee's general science, education and culture section to a department of its own, directly under the Party Secretariat. That same year, Castro marked a new departure with the publication of *Fidel and Religion*. While recognising the historical value of Marx's dictum that 'religion is the opium of the masses', he expressed the conviction that religion *per se* is neither opium nor miracle, and is only so insofar as it is used to defend either the oppressors and exploiters, or the oppressed and exploited. He went beyond the earlier notion of a strategic alliance between Christians and Marxists to one of unity, reminiscent of a previous idea of Che Guevara: that when Christians no longer allow religion to be used by the reactionaries of Latin America and instead take up the revolutionary challenge, then revolution will be invincible.

The Church hierarchy, especially that of the Catholic Church, is understandably more wary of the Marxist-Christian dialogue, and this reluctance to enter into the process of reconciliation has occasioned a certain amount of internal Church dissent. There is a whole generation of younger Church people who have grown up during the revolution, inculcated with both revolutionary and Christian values, which they see as coinciding on many points. This generation and its ecumenical movement has grown up defending revolution to the congregation and Christianity to communist militants. From the Salvation Army to the Reformed Christian Church, these young people speak a language that is a fusion of Marxist and Christian analysis, a little different from what one would expect of many of their Anglo-Saxon counterparts. They speak of evangelising society, not in the sense of any Gospel-preaching sect, but rather in terms of caring and doing, with none of the hypocrisy between professed beliefs and personal codes of conduct, whether they be Christian or communist. They see their Church and their religion as firmly situated in their society and needing to be part of the process of building a new, more ethical society.

Perhaps, it can be argued, the most important and exciting recent development of all in Cuba is coming from the young. With over half the population now under 30, that is, born within the revolution, there is a very definite generational gap. The young see their society and its problems in a very different light, questioning old symbols and cliches. While there is on the one hand a layer of youth apathy, especially in the city and tourist resort areas, there is also a militant youth making its voice heard. A strong spirit of analysis pervaded the Communist Youth Congress of spring 1987 and the even more youthful follow-up Intermediate Students Federation Congress the following December. The talk of the island was how constructively outspoken these young people were, challenging even Fidel Castro, in person, on a number of very concrete issues.

In a similar vein, in early summer 1988 young artists sparked off a quasi-philosophical debate on the state and civil society, which has also found expression in new music and dance forms. The new hit song of the country's most popular *salsa* group 'Los Van Van', entitled 'Nobody Loves Nobody', was originally conceived of as a love song. It then took on a life of its own as it was widely interpreted to be an indictment of certain attitudes in society which are more concerned for the individual than for the community.

The song came as a lighter sequel to a much-discussed polemical article on the 'excellence or excrescence' of certain modes of 'self-employed' work or 'services' offered. The article, published in the evening daily *Juventud Rebelde*, had been written by the party ideological secretary, Carlos Aldana. It was in response to a spate of letters that had been published by the paper on the subject, both for and against. He wrote:

> To discover the qualities of simple mercantile production and present an apologia for small-time higgling [to coin an appropriate Jamaican term] on the threshold of the third millenium and in the throes of such a colossal venture as a genuine socialist revolution, constitutes a sorry state of cultural and ideological poverty. To launch into it with all your guns is like using cannon against sparrows on the vegetable patch.

He went on to say:

> If there is any virtue in bringing this up again, it is because it brings to the fore one facet of the ideological struggle lying beneath the apparent placidness and unanimity in our society. Reflected as it has been in multiple ways, the struggle underlines the contrast between selfless, quiet heroism and examples of altruism and solidarity, and, at the other

23

extreme, gross, self-justifying individualism that is at times shamefully tolerated under the shield of errors and shortcomings we still have and the objective limitations to real economic development.

The article was a full-page feature in the newspaper, and not only reflected on various aspects of Cuba's current rectification campaign, but also pointed to the serious nature of ideological confrontation which is currently running through Cuban society. Explanations for problems, Aldana declared, did not end with the argument, irrefutable though it may be, of foreign aggression, permanent hostility, political siege, economic blockade, and — one might add — unfavourable trade relations in a world capitalist economic crisis. Cuba may no longer face many basic developmental problems common to other Latin American and Caribbean countries. However, within that, there are internal economic issues — as Aldana put it, shades of 'mediocrity, inefficiency and indolence' — that cannot be glossed over. These, he argued, help explain the lack of attention paid to certain personal and family needs within the macrosystem of state provision for health, education and subsistence, which had initially created the space for small-time lucrative gain.

June 1987 figures showed 50,000 people in Cuba registered as self-employed. These people rendered, Aldana conceded, necessary and socially useful services, ultimately of benefit to all. However, this did not mean having to condone the widespread dishonesty of inflated prices charged for an often substandard product. Nor did it preclude working towards genuine longer-term solutions, rooted in social production, that can provide a rational response to the multiple needs and aspirations of modern living. 'There can be no deifying the common leech', he pronounced.

The government is taking a hard line. Social production, seen to be state-owned, planned and controlled, is currently the paradigm. With the uneasy exception of farming cooperatives and small agricultural producers, anything else is little short of a 'capitalist formula', Castro has said. But, to what extent can the state plan and control an economy, especially one like that of Cuba, so dependent as it is on the export of primary agricultural produce and, subsequently, on foreign exchange? To what extent can people in general realistically behave in altruistic fashion after three decades of struggling, only partially successfully, to break out of that dependence? And, to what extent do people agree with current government policies, especially in Havana, which, in relation to the countryside, has been allowed to run down, and which, given its size, is where state bottlenecks in goods and services are most acute? Local consumer and service initiatives in some rural communities are filling the market gap, within state parameters, in a way that has no parallel in the city, although there is now a programme under way to revitalise the capital.

Support for most revolutions has come from expectations of improved living standards, and ultimately the scope and quality of goods and services available must influence public opinion. Eugenio Rodríguez Balari, head of Cuba's Market Research Institute, periodically reminds people that consumerism is not to be confused with luxury consumption. While the country needs a producer, not consumer, mentality, people also have legitimate consumer desires. Cuba may have stocked its shelves with cheap clothing and shoes accessible to all, if on ration, but now people want a better quality, more fashionable product. Cubans are on average two-radio households, and now require not Soviet, but superior Japanese radios. Moreover, even in the 'boom' period of 1981-4, social consumption might have risen by 7.1 per cent, but private consumption rose only by 2.5 per cent, and has since fallen drastically back. Improved standards on one level raise expectations on another. People are not necessarily any the less revolutionary for having such expectations, and the revolution has to recognise this and to find ways of responding.

Current development debates in both capitalist and socialist worlds centre on the 'rolling-back of the state'. Associated with this gradual diminution of central executive power are greater leeway for market forces and greater decentralisation in planning, as a backdrop to democratisation. From this perspective, the benefactor state is seen to present its own problems. It is unwieldy and top-heavy. It is also ultimately no more than the sum of the people that go to make it up, who may or may not be doing a good job.

The whole relationship between state and civil society, between individual and collective initiative within a just social ordering, is not easy under the best of circumstances. And Cuba is being put to the test today. The major question, as the revolution reaches its 30th anniversary, amidst internal and external difficulties, but with some strong alliances built up, must be how that relationship works itself out in such a way as to consolidate the very considerable social and political gains that have been made.

1. The Cooperative Hope

In 1983, Cuba's peasant farmers in Agricultural Production Cooperatives (CPAs) became the beneficiaries of a contributory scheme for state social security provision such as paid vacations, maternity benefits and pensions (based on a declared estimate of the number of years working the land). This was the first time peasant farmers had become recipients of government benefits on a par with state-salaried agricultural and industrial workers, some of whom had benefited from schemes that predated the revolution, others of whom had come under the wider umbrella of the revolutionary government's social security provision.

According to figures at the close of 1986, the state had laid out over 58 million pesos under the scheme on pensions alone, as over 35,000 CPA farmers had taken retirement. The fact that they did so created a major dislocation. Against the 58 million peso outlay, the state only brought in 25 million pesos through contributions, thereby creating a substantial deficit. Also, the relatively fledgling CPA movement was left with too much land, with insufficient labour to work it, exacerbating a trend whereby profitability margins were already being squeezed. By 1987, the National Association of Small Farmers (ANAP) was endorsing a government call for farmers not to retire if they were at all able to continue contributing their experience and know-how to agriculture, in part to guarantee production and in part to balance state finances. The result was that in early 1988 special measures were taken whereby all retirement requests were to be analysed carefully at the CPA and local ANAP offices and every attempt was to be made to persuade the farmer, wherever possible, to go on working. Periodic reports on the overall retirement/pensions situation were also to be made to regional and national ANAP offices, labour sections of People's Power Assemblies

27

at the various levels, and the national State Committee for Labour and Social Security.

When official doubts over pensions were first publicly aired at the 7th ANAP Congress in 1987, there was obvious consternation from several quarters. Not only those directly affected, that is, CPA farmers of retirement age, but many in society in general expressed a certain dismay. Social security was felt to be a central and growing gain of the revolution, and any attempt to limit it was perceived as a step backwards, perhaps all the more so because it came with a more general series of problems within the cooperative sector.

The issues were complex. An ageing peasantry taking what was seen as due retirement after a hard life on the land highlighted other problems facing the cooperatives. In 1983, Cuba was riding high on the success story of cooperatives. By 1986, many were beset by organisational difficulties and fewer and fewer were proving to be profitable as diseconomies of scale set in, especially in labour-intensive crops for which mechanisation was not an option, such as fresh vegetables, tobacco and coffee.

Hopes had been pinned for over a decade on the CPAs being able, with state support, to spearhead more localised development programmes. The way in which the cooperatives were conceived, on an autonomous, voluntary, highly participatory basis, augured well, many felt, not only for equity but also for democratisation within the process of rural decision-making. However, the extent to which they would perform this role depended on many factors, including their measure of economic viability.

What makes developments in the peasant sector over the last few years particularly interesting, is how economic efficiency and equity have been in the balance, in the context of structures that have been created for people to give greater voice to their own concerns as to the kind of action that should be taken. This has included not only hard appraisals of cooperative ventures but also the less economically successful state-run farms and overly profiteering small farmers.

Old farmers who had joined the cooperatives questioned the wisdom of inexperienced volunteer and student labour, especially in more delicate crops and areas with little tradition of large-scale waged farming. 'You sometimes wonder whether it is outright sabotage of the revolution', a 62-year-old Villa Clara tobacco grower commented in 1984 on some of the devastating effects on state tobacco leaf grown in his area. 'State farm workers had the worst of both worlds: working the land but not getting food from it'. The same farmer would take off his straw hat and wipe his brow, venturing a 'difficult to say', when asked about who would work the cooperative's land in the future. His son was studying to be a translator in East Germany and his daughter was a teacher in the nearby town. He also pondered the tolerance of the revolution turning a blind eye to those little farm oases, whose owners had played the market right and at illicitly inflated prices bought their own water and electricity supplies, appliances and cars.

When a sombre-faced Castro walked into the major annual cooperative meeting in May 1986, he took with him some strong criticisms of the cooperative movement. By the end of the meeting, however, they had been met fairly and squarely with cooperative farmers' criticisms of both the free farmers' markets and state farming mechanisms. The immediate shut-down of the markets and longer-term rethinking of state agricultural policy ever since have to be seen in this context. They are developments that can hardly be understood without reference to historic and geographical issues that Cuba has faced in its agrarian transition.

Rural versus Rural: the Development Context

An anomaly of contemporary Cuba is that, while the economy is still based primarily on export agriculture, less than 30 per cent of the population is defined as rural. This is not simply because much of agriculture is large-scale mechanised sugar-cane growing or land-extensive cattle-grazing, although these factors play a part. Nor is it due to mere census definitions, for these respond in large measure to changing development realities. Cuba classifies as 'urban' any settlement that has 2,000 or more inhabitants, but also settlements with a population of 500-2,000 if they have electricity, running water, education and health facilities, as well as new towns of 200-500 inhabitants with those same amenities. The census definitions, that is to say, are based less on numerical size than on the public services attached to a given community.

The phenomenon behind the definition has been called one of 'rural urbanisation' and was part of the revolutionary government's package to raise rural work and living standards, understood to include housing, health and education services. Rural urbanisation was seen as a way of providing small rural communities with the economic, social and cultural amenities associated with urban life. By 1975, a total of 282 new communities had been built by the state as part of integral regional socio-economic development plans in sugar and other cash crops, cattle-raising and the like. Since then, state support for individual farmers to form farming cooperatives can be seen as an extension of that early policy of rural urbanisation, with greater emphasis on self-sufficiency and self-help in building similar local communities.

A particular concern has been expressed for the social and economic development of Cuba's more inaccessible and isolated mountain areas. These districts, traditionally neglected by pre-revolutionary governments, were where the rural poor had been driven to subsistence agriculture by land-grabbing lowland estates. Attempts to redress that trend by the revolutionary government had been overshadowed by the greater attractions of regional development plans in more lowland parts, causing an exodus that was most detrimental to the mountain coffee-growing economy. Special state policies of the mid to late 1980s were designed to counter the demographic trend. The highly popular Family Doctor programme — the most recent phase in mass health care provisions at the community level that now covers many urban and rural districts — started in precisely those mountainous areas. The young counsellor-doctors started their rounds on horseback, riding the hills of the Sierra Maestra range where rebel forces had once ridden before. They did so in areas where, 30 years on, health indices were much improved but still higher than the national average for crucial indicators such as fertility, and infant and maternal mortality.

A number of studies pointed to the need for prioritising resources to meet basic infrastructural needs still lacking in cut-off areas: electricity, running water, sanitation, housing, and more accessible schools, roads, and transport. Some of these could be met on a fairly local level by mobilising cooperatives to help build homes and other facilities. Others such as roads and mini-hydroelectric dams required a rechanneling of state construction activity away from other development areas.

It has been a basic tenet of government policy over the last 30 years to push through development programmes that are designed to help narrow, rather than widen, the rural/urban and rural/rural divides, that is, for programmes to have an equalising effect in 'humanising' the countryside. This has inevitably meant a certain drop in standards in city and traditionally more prosperous rural parts, but has produced a definite upgrading of more deprived areas. Even so, the process of upgrading has not been easy in mountain and more remote lowland areas relegated to poor peasant agriculture in the past, as these have fallen outside the scope of state-controlled plans.

What initially paved the way for large-scale rural change was a sweeping land reform. In the market economy of 20th-century pre-revolutionary Cuba, much traditional farming had been disrupted by large-scale foreign and local capital investment. This was particularly true of sugar plantation agriculture and land-extensive cattle-ranching and held to a lesser degree for tobacco and other branches of agriculture. Nowhere, however, had it ushered in any uniform agricultural modernisation. On the contrary, it had often served to strengthen archaic forms of production, with significant variations from sector to sector. Operating alongside modern farming units with salaried labourers was small-scale, labour-intensive, small tenant and subtenant farming and sharecropping. Despite rather misleading 1953 census figures quoting some 60 per cent of the 'economically active population' in agriculture as wage labour, there was in fact a very considerable semi-peasantry/semi-proletariat which farmed small plots of land according to intricate systems of land tenure and rent-in-kind, was highly dependent on unpaid family labour, and was forced, at different times of the year, to sell its labour.

In this way, local and foreign capital often owned the land (73.3 per cent of the land was in the hands of 9.4 per cent of landholders), but preferred to use credit and buying mechanisms rather than farm the land directly. On the one hand, large tracts of land might be left idle; in 1959, it has been estimated, only 23.6 per cent of cultivable land was actually utilised. On the other, the drive to accumulate capital was through landlords renting and subrenting their land and through complex systems of sharecropping, which usually required sharecroppers to hand over one-fifth, one-quarter, or one-third of the crop. Male agricultural work was accompanied by intensified women's participation in subsistence production and family reproduction crucial to family survival, plus the seasonal harvesting and sorting of tobacco; and child farm labour was common from the age of about seven years upwards. A largely white peasant-proletariat could, moreover, be supplemented by tapping a reserve army of mostly black, migrant, landless labour.

The letting, subletting and sharecropping of land is crucial to any understanding of labour and poverty at the bottom of the pecking order in pre-revolutionary Cuba. Depending on the land tenure system, growers could be particularly vulnerable to landowners, creditors, buyers and the many middlemen and speculators. Large absentee landowners would have managers for parts of their farms and allocate more outlying parts to sharecropping. Most would call on paid or unpaid tenant farmer or sharecropper labour for other services and had their own local stores which functioned on credit and pay chits. In this way, owners and managers bore little risk for agricultural production, especially in the more delicate crop areas, or for unstable markets. Little wonder that land tenure was seen as

31

the single most important factor in the revolution's programme for improving rural life.

The May 1959 Agrarian Reform Law, substantially implemented by the summer of 1960, put a 400 hectare ceiling on private land ownership. Land in excess of the maximum holding was either given in units of not more than 67 hectares to small landless tillers (tenant, subtenant and sharecropping farmers) or turned into state farms. Taken along with nationalisation of foreign and large-scale domestic enterprise (1960-61), the reform meant the effective appropriation of large landed estates (especially sugar and cattle). In May 1961, the National Association of Small Farmers was set up to group together all private farmers holding up to 400 hectares of land. However, overt political hostility on the part of the middle agrarian bourgeoisie (for example in tobacco), untouched by this first law, plus an observable depreciation of property and capital in agriculture, motivated the 2nd Agrarian Reform Law of 1963, which reduced the ceiling on all private land to 67 hectares.

Roughly speaking, the first law affected 70 per cent of agricultural land, of which 40 per cent became state-controlled and 30 per cent

---

Permanent Production Brigades

In the late 1960s everyone was doing voluntary work. The ten million ton sugar harvest effort had accountants and university professors wielding machetes for days and weeks on end. In the early 1970s whole workplaces would be out by the truckload at the weekend to tend coffee, weed potatoes and gather tomatoes, to the point of great jams blocking access roads and more time being spent getting there and back than actually in the field. The schools in the countryside eased up the need for voluntary labour in many non-sugar areas, and by the late 1980s it had almost been phased out. Instead, remaining labour needs, where mechanisation was not possible in sugar and for labour-intensive harvesting such as tobacco, were met by permanent production brigades. Still in operation today, they operate seasonally, drawing on highly productive workers for a given crop. They might be former peasant farmers or agricultural labourers now working in other spheres, or might have had no agricultural background, but excelled when they put their hand to it. In a situation where there is endemic seasonal demand in agriculture, it is a way of attempting to maximise productivity within the cost restraints of mobilising large numbers, at their regular salary levels, plus transport and accommodation.

was placed in the hands of the small peasantry, leaving the remaining 30 per cent in the hands of a middle peasantry. This last was eliminated under the second, more radical land reform. By the late 1960s the sale or rental of private land to the state had resulted in an 80:20 per cent ratio of state to private agricultural land, and the ratio today is approximately 85:15 per cent. In numerical terms, in the late 1960s, there were 400,000 agricultural labourers on state farms as against 250,000 ANAP members. Today the balance is all the more tilted towards the state sector, with 700,000 and 180,000 respectively. However, in practice, just as before the revolution, the categories of state farm worker and small farmer have never been as neat as may have appeared. Many small farmers were, from the very early years, involved in mutual aid organisations that were given explicit support through ANAP. Peasant associations (ACs) were the most loosely organised variant, emerging originally out of pre-revolutionary struggles against peasant eviction. Credit and service cooperatives (CCSs) were a more structured attempt to organise agricultural inputs and services on a collective basis. Agricultural societies (SAs) were a further step towards actually pooling the land in the early 1960s. All helped to modify traditional peasant relations of production. Conversely, state farm workers privately tended illicitly syphoned-off small plots for subsistence production. There were also constant mobilisations of casual and seasonal labour, both paid and voluntary, from state to private sectors, and vice-versa, making for a continued, if irregular, fluidity of labour.

Whatever the continuity and changes in farming and labour patterns, agriculture was the keystone for ambitious, and at times over-ambitious, state plans, normally centred on Cuba's traditional export crop — sugar. In the early 1960s, there was an initial attempt to break with sugar dependency and diversify towards alternative exports and increased domestic production. It was a costly mistake, for diversification could not compensate for the financial collapse of sugar. A change in policy in 1963 looked to sugar again as the springboard for future, longer-term diversification of agriculture and industry, with growing import substitution and self-sufficiency. This was to be backed by securing favourable bilateral and multilateral trading agreements with the socialist bloc, with indexed prices on a sliding scale.

With the return to sugar, the swift transition to socialist forms of post-revolutionary agrarian organisation reflected in large measure the earlier process of agricultural development, characterised by specialised commercial farming. And yet, even in sugar, Cuba's most modernised crop, semi-proletarianisation and lack of technology

33

served to hold back the successful later development of state farms. It was not until the 1980s that even modern agro-industrial sugar complexes had anywhere near the conditions as regards technification and mechanisation to offset the considerable investment outlay and raised labour and social costs needed to be run as profitable concerns, and a great many are still as yet unprofitable.

The predominance of state-appropriated lands, dominated by the sugar and cattle sectors, led to a perception of state farms as the model for socialist agriculture. This was as true for dairy and poultry farming as for other crops such as rice, tubers, citrus fruit, bananas, tomatoes and peppers. In the rush of development plans in the 1960s

---

Sugar

Sugar-cane growing in Cuba dates back to the 1500s, and by the late 16th century, growing demand in Europe had led to increasing production and export of sugar, along with coffee and tobacco, to Spain. A significant boost to European demand came with the industrial revolution at the turn of the 19th century, coinciding with pressures to relax colonial controls and the elimination of Cuba's considerable rival producer Haiti, with the Haitian revolution. The tremendous growth of a slave-based agro-industrial sugar economy up until the 1880s, and an increasingly industrially technified one after the mid-century, created strong racial, pro-Spanish planter interests. Juxtaposed as they were with free trade economic philosophy, since more and more of the 19th century island's trade and investment was first with Britain and then with the US, nationalist and abolitionist sentiment was late developing relative to the rest of hispanic America, making Cuba one of the last to end slavery (1886) and colonial rule (1898).

The sugar mono-producing export economy really came into its own in the first quarter of the 20th century with massive US investment in production for export to the US, giving rise to huge sugar mill complexes on vast expanses of land, generating great financial wealth at one end of the scale and a cheap reserve of seasonal labour at the other. From 1926, US and European protectionism for their own beet sugar undercut world cane markets and therefore the mainstay of Cuba's economy. Although there were some signs of increasing cane sugar demand in the 1950s, the revolution basically inherited a cane sector (and by extension a whole economy) in crisis, with resulting endemic unemployment and impoverishment in the countryside.

When the US cut its sugar quota yet again in retaliation for the revolutionary government's nationalisation programme, the USSR

---

to revitalise agriculture as well as industry, and provide health, education and other services, these farms generated a great need for large-scale voluntary, as well as paid, labour. In the 1970s, the farms were also attached to new secondary schools in the countryside, which espoused combined study-work programmes to boost agricultural production.

The drive to double the mid-1960s annual sugar crop (some 80 per cent state-controlled) to the ten million ton mark by 1970 and the priority given to the impressive number of both sugar and non-sugar state farms throughout the 1960s inevitably had its negative repercussions on private-sector farming. This held as much for export

stepped in with an offer to buy on advantageous terms for Cuba. The rationale of getting the most out of sugar to spearhead more diversified development was taken to such extremes as to produce the all-out effort for the 1970 ten million ton harvest (in the event 8.5 million) and to over-extend commitments on high mid-1970s Western European market prices. The price Cuba had to pay for both, but more particularly its dominant trading relationship with the USSR in place of the US, has been termed the new dependency.

The Latin American dependency school highlighted the extraction of economic surplus from less to more developed countries by diverse mechanisms of 'exploitation' or 'unequal exchange'. The USSR, by contrast, is generally agreed to supply a subsidy to, rather than extract a surplus from, the economy of Cuba. The new dependency criterion applied to contemporary Cuba, is rather derived from its opposite: 'external economic interdependence', that is, an economy's ability to meet its own needs, which Cuba was clearly in no position to do. It inherited a whole sugar infrastructure which it reasoned could be used positively under an international theory of comparative advantage working in its favour.

Internal linkages were sought whereby the expansion of sugar went hand-in-hand with increasing 'independence' of the industry for its inputs in the form of energy self-sufficiency (bagasse), machinery and equipment (home-built combine harvesters for mechanisation and therefore humanisation of labour) and production (a considerable by-products industry in the form of cattle-feed, bagasse-board for construction, and pharmaceuticals). However, massive Soviet inputs have obscured levels of economic inefficiency behind the very obvious gains and these will have to be ironed out both internally and with regard to external trading patterns.

crops such as tobacco (75 per cent privately farmed and with a 66 per cent drop in harvests over 1965-70) as for small-scale farming for domestic consumption (where the drop was significantly alarming, albeit not quite as drastic as in tobacco). This led to pressures from ANAP, from its 4th Congress in 1971, for a revaluation of the role of small private farming.

From the start of the revolution, small farmers had benefited from state credit and pricing policies and certain rural extension services channeled through their various incipient forms of association. In 1963, 346 agricultural societies and 587 credit and service cooperatives had been formed. However, by 1967, the number of societies had fallen to 136, and to 41 by 1971, although that same year the number of credit and service cooperatives had grown to 1,119.

The drop in the number of societies had been clearly related to the policy priority for sugar and the state farm model, and the 1970s ushered in a period of greater state attention to other branches of agriculture and their corresponding private-sector farms. As 1963 saw a swing back to sugar, so the years 1971-6 were defined as a period of 'tobacco recuperation', with sweeping price reforms and agricultural research and extension for local crops. It would take another decade for a similarly sweeping programme to be pushed through for coffee and fresh vegetables. In the 1970s, several new agricultural research stations and agricultural institutes were opened, and the emphasis was on developing new crop strains and breeding stock, soil improvement, irrigation, fertiliser and pesticides, and technification where possible, all of which was made available to both the state and private sector. In the case of the latter, ANAP, as well as the Ministry of Agriculture, allocated resources and provided technical personnel.

The application of technical know-how was facilitated by generally improved educational standards in rural areas. Out of the literacy campaign of the early 1960s came continuing adult education programmes, some under the auspices of the Ministry of Education, others run by mass organisations such as ANAP or the Federation of Cuban Women (FMC), through the FMC-ANAP brigades. A current major adult education drive has encouraged state agricultural workers (like their industrial counterparts) and ANAP members to complete 9th-grade education. In addition to the Ministry of Agriculture's extension services, ANAP has its own team of agronomists and local para-professionals, through whom there has evolved a whole technical activist movement. The extension agents encourage farmers and farm workers to come forward with innovations and to be on the alert for crop diseases. This last has

36

been especially important in preventive crop control in both state and private sectors since the early 1980s, when there were major blights of sugar-cane rust, tobacco blue mould and coffee smut (suspiciously all simultaneously decimating crops after many years of non-incidence, in much the same way as the CIA-introduced African swine fever virtually wiped out the pig population in the early 1970s).

Over the years, the cost of natural disasters such as hurricanes, flooding and drought was absorbed by the state through a cancellation of debts on credits and material and financial assistance for reconstruction. A more recent development has been the introduction of an extensive low-cost agricultural insurance scheme, on a more contributory basis. And, when the 1977 ANAP Congress announced its support for a pronounced pooling of private land and resources in the form of the CPAs, the cooperative movement was also envisaged in a contributory vein, through which the state would levy a certain amount of end-of-year earnings in return for its support and services. This marked a new departure in agricultural thinking, and one that was beginning to be applied to the state sector as well. For the questions this and other aspects of the cooperative movement have since raised, both for the cooperative sector itself and cooperative relations *vis-a-vis* the state and the individual private sector, it is worth considering that movement in more detail.

Rural Democracy

The new CPAs were aimed at modernising the remaining dispersed, labour-intensive private sector through land concentration and technification. It was also hoped that, with the growth of new cooperative communities, it would be economically more viable to break the social isolation of poorer peasant homes. It was a two-pronged, social as much as economic, policy. At the same time, the new state economic management and planning system of the late 1970s set out to combine national planning priorities with greater decentralisation of decision-making, local initiative and agricultural self-sufficiency in the state sector. In effect, a certain convergence could be noted between state farms and cooperatives as the former were also encouraged to function as enterprises which had a degree of autonomy in self-management, utilised a percentage of end-of-year revenue for enterprise and local development, and encouraged subsistence food production as much as cash crop efficiency.

The CPAs were a more carefully organised variant of the attempts during the 1960s to pool private holdings in the form of agricultural societies. The remaining few such societies set the example by

The State Model

Key theoretical concepts on the transition to socialist agriculture are the nationalisation of land, the development of large-scale scientific farming, and the socialisation of production with a rural proletariat. Based on observations of capitalist development, they envisage replacing planning for market forces, with an equitable and efficient allocation of resources and growth of output. The worker-peasant alliance is a recognition of the incomplete and uneven process of capitalist development in countries undergoing socialist transition.

Cuba is one of the few small Third World countries to have experienced such levels of capitalist development of pre-revolutionary agriculture as to have undertaken a sweeping nationalisation programme as part of socialist transformation. Preconceived economies of scale in the agro-export economy of sugar and cattle go a long way to explain the revolutionary governments' preference for not dividing up the land and operating state farms as the predominant form of production.

Early internal reasons for operating large estates as state farms rather than cooperatives was the fear that heterogeneous production conditions and productivity of estates would lead to severe inequalities among rich and poor cooperatives; that cooperatives run by permanent workers would not address seasonal employment of temporary workers and exacerbate income inequalities among the workforce; and that cooperatives would conceivably contribute to growing tensions between capitalist producers and the state. External reasons involved the USSR and attractive sugar agreements, whereby advantageous prices for sugar could be used for financing development in other areas.

Constraints proved to be the excessive priority given to cash crop sugar exports, causing Cuba to be caught up in a continuing imported foodstuffs/domestic production dilemma. With the exception of sugar, cattle, some roots and fruits, few economies of scale were operative and social gains were becoming an obstacle to economic performance in terms of labour costs and motivation. The result was low productivity in the predominantly export/cash crop state sector and underutilisation of the increasingly smaller, largely domestic production peasant sector, though peasant farming productivity was as high, if not higher, than the state.

The 1975 Party Congress was a major turning point in recognising peasant cooperatives also as a superior form of production, although state farms were still considered the more advanced, given that theoretically they represented ownership by all the people and the wealth generated by them went to benefit the whole of society.

becoming cooperatives. The peasant associations and credit cooperatives out of which other CPAs grew were already versed in acting collectively on behalf of individual farmers; the land might still have been worked individually, but peasant associations and credit cooperatives negotiated agreements on state quotas for production, inputs and credits.

In the CPAs, land and other basic means of production (such as tractors, other vehicles, tools, buildings, inputs, etc) are owned by the farmers' collective, as opposed to the state, and each individual farmer's contribution is valued and paid off over a period of time from funds set aside by the cooperatives expressly for this purpose. The cooperative is farmed and run collectively as an autonomous enterprise within the constraints of national and regional planning. It receives low interest credits from the state and preferential treatment in the allocation of certain resources. A percentage of profits goes to the state in return for services, a percentage is turned back for production and amenities, and the rest is divided among members, according to their labour contribution. The cooperative elects its own president and executive committee and meets in full once a month. At a major end-of-year meeting, production plans, investment programmes, and consumption requirements are decided upon, as well as such issues as advance pay, profit-sharing and the admission of new members.

Individual farmers not wishing to join a cooperative formed in a given region are not pressured to do so. Conversely, agricultural labourers — and, in exceptional cases, even industrial workers — may join the cooperatives. In such cases, they contribute nothing other than labour and hence receive no compensation for machinery and inputs, although these members do have statutory rights identical to those of other cooperative farmers. The same applies to landless wives and grown children of male heads of household.

It was envisaged that once the first few cooperatives were organised, their greater social and economic advantages would be widely recognised, and that others would soon be formed. The cooperative movement did in fact mushroom, agricultural output doubled and tripled in early years, and the number of cooperatives and membership grew to a rapid peak in 1983. Since then, the number has dropped for various reasons. By a logical progression, growth rates could be expected to taper off, but fusions have also led to a smaller number of CPAs with an increased average land size. Membership also fell from 82,000 in 1983 to 68,000 in 1987, in part reflecting people leaving the cooperatives but also the fact that older members were retiring. On 1987 figures, there were some 1,400

CPAs, holding over one million hectares of land, accounting for over 60 per cent of total peasant landholdings.

State-cooperative relations have been chequered, at the national as well as a more local level. Early successes in the cooperative sector in some cases rivalled and emphasised deficient state-sector performance. State distribution agencies of agricultural inputs and know-how can be argued to have had an in-built bias towards servicing the state sector first, especially when supplies were running short. On the cooperative side, 'illicit' labour practices and extra-agricultural activities were seen to be contributing to untoward profit, putting the pressure on other less economically viable cooperatives to follow suit. This became a more and more tempting prospect as profit margins began to drop, thereby leaving state farms and state farm workers at a definite disadvantage in comparison with the peasant sector. To this had to be added the negative impact of lucrative farmer and middleman speculation, in conjunction with certain informal sharecropping arrangements contributing to

---

Cooperatives and Rectification

'The peasants were also getting corrupted. We no longer knew if a cooperative was an Agricultural Production Cooperative, an arts and crafts cooperative, an industrial cooperative, a commercial cooperative, or a middleman's cooperative. We were losing our sense of order; the trading between the cooperatives and the state enterprises, state enterprises exchanging products, materials, foodstuffs among themselves, like the case Raúl [Castro] mentioned yesterday of a factory exchanging products with a farm, because while it sent the agricultural cooperative cement sweepings, the agricultural enterprise sent salted meat and who knows what else to the cement factory.

If everyone started doing that, if that proliferated, nothing would be left. There wouldn't be any meat for the schools, for the hospitals, for what has to be distributed to the population every day, every week, every month. If this kind of generalised trading developed among the state enterprises or between the Agricultural Production Cooperatives and state enterprises, no one knows where this would all end, in what kind of chaos and anarchy. These are evident negative tendencies, extremely evident!'

Fidel Castro, Speech to deferred session of 3rd Congress of the Cuban Communist Party, 2 December 1986. Printed in *New International*, No 6, 1987.

---

enrichment in the individual farming sector, let alone a growing phenomenon of syphoned-off state resources used to play the market. The net result was the May 1986 2nd National Meeting of CPAs which called for a clampdown on non-state marketing procedures and improved state-cooperative relations.

State versus Market

Effected as it was almost overnight, the closure of non-state markets for agricultural produce added to the problems of an already deficient state marketing system and was but the beginnings of a major state headache. Lucrative market operations might have stimulated small farmers to grow extra produce to help meet market demand and also to travel often quite considerable distances to market, but they had also occasioned all kinds of spin-off phenomena, such as state produce also finding its way there, with instances of state-employed truck drivers bearing illicit bananas for this purpose from one end of the island to the other. If production and consumption levels were to be maintained without this other kind of activity, state distribution mechanisms had to be stepped up to fill the gap. Immediately, this meant vehicles to transport produce, and these vehicles had to be procured abroad, at considerable cost, it might be said, given the urgency with which they were needed. More importantly, in the longer term, broader relations between the state, the cooperative sector and the individual small farmer needed to be worked out.

Germs of the current government position could be seen back in 1982 at the 6th ANAP Congress, but the strongest formulation was produced at the 2nd National CPAs Meeting in 1986, the 7th ANAP Congress in 1987 and the 3rd National CPAs Meeting in 1988. The general policy thrust has been largely endorsed by ANAP, although there clearly remains much discussion concerning particular policies and problems, as seen from local and provincial ANAP meetings throughout 1988.

Among the various possible avenues of action considered in the early 1980s was an agricultural tax. Farmers were understandably opposed to the measure and it was temporarily postponed, especially since the initial outlay in levying the tax, whether on land, production, sales or profits, across the board or on a sliding scale, would inevitably outweigh monies collected. Another proposal at the time was that all sellers should be certified by ANAP as having met their state quotas. This was intended to give market access only to legitimate small farm produce, and not that coming from syphoned-off plots and from state enterprises.

A 1986 report to a meeting of municipal agricultural officials working with the peasant farming sector was particularly eloquent on the situation created. The attempt to boost production through the private market had not been accompanied by sufficient thinking through of agrarian relations of production, it was argued, as further details were released. By 1985, the peasant sector was producing in all 21 per cent of total agricultural production, varying from 12 per cent of milk production, 19 per cent of sugar, through 25 per cent of cattle, 26 per cent of citrus and other fruits, to 60 per cent of cacao and 73 per cent of tobacco. Of 562.5 million pesos of peasant sector production, 258.3 million were produced by the CPAs and 304.2 million by the credit and service cooperatives. That is to say, the credit cooperatives produced 54 per cent of the sector's value on one third less land than that occupied by the CPAs. Put another way, for every 50 target units of production per CPA member, the figure met was 37; for every 32 target units per credit cooperative member, the figure met was 47. Since there were some 14,000 CPAs with close to 70,000 members, as against 2,000 credit cooperatives with 100,000 members and 269 peasant associations with 10,000 members, it was also clear that the CPAs had half the labour power per hectare.

In 1985, an inspection of 600 CPAs concluded that free trading was rapidly fomenting rural social differentiation, and more particularly, a *nouveau riche* peasantry, to the detriment of CPA growth and performance. It had led to plots and small farms springing up on privately owned land in what were termed 'illicit' subletting and sharecropping arrangements. ANAP, which was considered to be a truly mass organisation of peasant farmers, proved to have none of these plots on its register. Also, the CPAs had responded to decreasing membership by looking to contract labour, thereby raising labour costs and lowering earnings, rather than seeking increased internal productivity.

It was on the strength of this report that the 1986 2nd National CPAs Meeting was called to account. As a result, that meeting addressed a whole series of irregularities within both the cooperative and individual farm sector such as illegal tenure of land, idle farm land, excessive use of hired labour, sharecropping and illicit sales. During the next year a programme of measures was drawn up to deal with these, focusing on contractual and monetary arrangements between cooperatives and state enterprises, and state as well as ANAP extension work with the cooperative sector.

Economic efficiency had been deteriorating across the board, such that average production costs of 64 cents to the peso in 1980 were up to 82 cents by 1985, when 30 per cent of CPAs were not breaking even, as against only 11 per cent in 1982. As a result, special attention has been paid to factors affecting profitability, which in itself has contributed to farmers leaving cooperatives. These factors have ranged from dispersed lands, poor soil preparation, plant strains and animal breeds, and overplanting and overcropping, to lack of managerial and financial experience, work days of four to five hours, working weeks of three or four days, poorly set work norms and food consumption levels, overinvestment and poor maintenance of farm equipment, and credit overcommitment on loans for housing construction. The exacerbation of many of these difficulties in mountainous areas and the proportionately higher cost of investment outlays has occasioned particular policies for mountain cooperatives, such as greater state infrastructure inputs, cancelling of interest on bank credits and taxes, and price increases for coffee and cacao, the basic crops.

If government was quick to find fault with internal cooperative workings, ANAP as an organisation and cooperative members have riposted by pointing out deficient state mechanisms and contractual arrangements which affect their functioning. The 7th ANAP Congress laid squarely at the door of the Ministry of Agriculture, Ministry of Sugar, Central Planning Board (JUCEPLAN) and other central state administrative agencies a lack of priorities in important decisions and coordination of resources for the cooperatives. Similarly, several examples could be given in this respect from 1988 municipal and provincial ANAP meetings, many of which were reported on extensively in the monthly ANAP magazine which goes out to all members. 'There should be an extra clause in contracts making allowances in delivery of quotas for lack of fertiliser or other supplies,' said Alberto Rogelio Lugo from La Plata CPA, at the Jagüey Grande, Matanzas province, meeting in early 1988. Exact quantities and regular delivery dates should also be stipulated, he argued. A similar meeting in Güira de Melena, Havana province, pointed to deficiencies in supplies, citing the lack of crates for harvesting produce as an example.

In several of its articles during 1988, the ANAP magazine referred to factors such as excessive pricing and charges for state supplies and services, and faulty pricing and weighing mechanisms on produce, detected in spot checks by the State Committee for Prices. In this case, the message was for cooperatives to be better informed and to keep invoices and receipts for any claims to be made, since money lost in this way could affect end-of-year accounts.

At the same time, there has been ample discussion of concrete examples of good functioning and malfunctioning within the cooperative sector. To cite instances of the latter, problems of a technical nature, such as insufficient irrigation or poor planting and overplanting were common. One CPA lost 80,000 pesos because it took a new agronomist at his word and allowed what turned out to be a disastrous experiment on 130 hectares of rice land. The same cooperative estimated that it had lost 20,000 pesos through poor labour discipline. At the Antonio Goitizolo CPA in Rodas, Cienfuegos province, it was estimated that poor labour discipline amounted to 5,000 working days lost in the year. One cooperative member complained that the average 19.2 days worked in the month should come as no surprise when, alongside those working 30 days, there were others who only worked 15. The Niceto Pérez CPA in Ranchuelo, Villa Clara province, was another at which there were complaints that some members were not pulling their weight, although this cooperative does run at a profit.

One aspect of the cooperative situation to which attention is already being drawn is the failure of women to come forward in the way that was hoped. It was very clear at the beginning of the cooperative movement that women, possibly more than the men, were pressing for the new facilities that went with cooperative development. Many women also became fully-fledged cooperative members. However, numbers have dwindled in relative, if not absolute terms, with current figures showing 15,000 women cooperative members, fewer than 25 per cent of the total and contributing only 12 per cent of the work time. Women comprise one-third of the technical force, and 13 per cent of CPA executive committee members are women. Recent regional meetings of cooperative women, from Guantánamo to Havana, have raised the obstacles that they face within the cooperative movement, not least the attitudes of their men, and have stressed the need for nurseries, training courses and cultural and recreational activities. An interesting new element has been the many women family doctors and nurses taking an active interest in cooperative life, as well as the medical problems of their patients.

Over the last few years, specially created Ministry of Agriculture and Ministry of Sugar sections have been working closely with ANAP and the farmers from the national to the local level, helping to establish tighter controls. ANAP itself has introduced instructors at the local level whose function is to see closely to cooperative needs, and there will be an ANAP secretary on every CPA executive committee. While not divested of its economic functions, ANAP is for the time being seen more as the political and educational organisation which it was originally set up to be.

The net positive effect has been a certain observable reanimation within the cooperative movement. In 1987, a trend was reversed as a total of 70 new CPAs were formed, with a growth in land area of over 30,000 hectares and 2,000 new members. Of the total of 1,418 CPAs, 897 were profitable in 1987, while many others were estimated to be on the verge of becoming so. Those that were unprofitable were functioning under special banking provisions and with special systematic checks and controls. Altogether, 254 university graduates and 1,269 middle-level technicians were working on the cooperatives, although 1,000 were still without a university professional and another 500 without a technician. Over two-thirds had access to electricity.

It is still too early to say how significant this upswing is, for there are as yet many factors unresolved. The irony of the decade 1975-85 was that a whole movement designed to upgrade the least developed had in fact created relative enrichment. As the *nouveau riche* emerged on the market scene, a typical comment in city queues was: 'so this is the worker-peasant alliance?' However, it also shook up a slothful state sector and encouraged it to improve its own performance. The dilemma for the state currently is that the desired order of economic efficiency is in reverse: individual peasant production can show a better performance than cooperative and cooperative better than state farm. Given the already tense present economic conditions facing the state nationally and internationally, it is difficult to see how that order can be changed very substantially in the near future without affecting overall economic levels.

There may well be a retrenchment in individual, and possibly cooperative, peasant sector production as controls set in, without any immediate compensatory effects from other quarters. By way of example, increased production can do little good if it is not met with increased distribution, and poor distribution has always been a known flaw in the state sector. Peasant farmers, as much as the population at large, have their own opinions on this and can make their position felt. In the end, limitations of this nature could ultimately force the state to swing the pendulum back to a more flexible market situation, as a matter of both economic and political expediency.

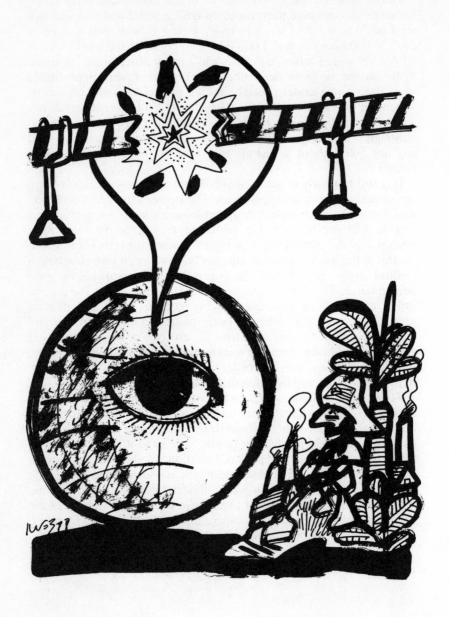

2. Money and Motivation

Whether as a means of interpreting reality or as a form of social engineering, model constructing is a precarious business. Almost invariably, the model depends on a certain equilibrium of forces that in the real world are constantly in flux. Ultimate success in the desired direction depends very much on the ability of the model to adjust to new forces and new elements of change. Each new change can modify those forces, in often unforeseen ways, that can never sufficiently accommodate the human factor involved in both individual and collective behavioural patterns and thought processes. It follows that a commendable policy based on what might seem to be a sound model can lead to steps that can falter, if not flounder. Cuban politicians and economists have found this to their cost. It is only thanks to a certain pragmatism that there has usually been a last minute change of direction. It has been interesting, and at times painful, to see this process in action since the current rectification campaign began, though it is too early to tell whether this particular change in direction will be successful or not.

At one of the lengthy televised meetings of union, management and party that marked the outset of the rectification campaign in 1986, on this occasion in the eastern province of Santiago de Cuba, there was a lively exchange between a worker delegate and President Castro on the subject of housing. The worker was from a huge new textile plant, one of various factory complexes that had been built outside town and city in designated new development areas. The plant was still only working at around 40 per cent of potential capacity, and one of the major problems it was facing was a high turnover of the work force. The worker argued that the main reason for the factory's inability to keep labour was that people had to travel long distances on poor transport and that housing close to the factory would go a long way towards solving the problem. The prospect of housing would also attract new labour and help ease the housing needs of the city of Santiago itself. Castro argued that this was all well and good, but asked where the money was going to come from, if not from production. It was a 'chicken and egg' problem, he conceded, but insisted that in the circumstances production had to come first. The worker held his ground, arguing that it would be impossible to raise production if social problems of this nature were not addressed quickly. Six months later, Castro was arguing the same thing and the country was embarked on a massive new state housing drive along revived microbrigade lines, linking workplace to construction site.

The Planned Economy

Cuban planning has a chequered history. During the early 1960s, an unsuccessful attempt to set up a centralised system along lines similar to that of Czechoslovakia was followed by a prolonged debate (1963-6) and then what has been considered as the Guevarist system in which the formal five-year plan framework was discarded. Mini-plans based on priority sectors or regions were predominant and were not coordinated at the national level. In the context of an economy attempting to survive political and military threat and tight economic blockade, decisions were taken largely by the political leadership and not the Central Planning Board (JUCEPLAN), and, in times of austerity, moral rather than material incentives were called into play.

The easing of external tensions plus the build-up to, and subsequent failure of, the 1970 sugar harvest, with its significant dislocation of agriculture and industry, led to the introduction of various measures to rationalise what had been an essentially siege or command economy. Greater overall planning, coupled with greater flexibility, channels for participation, and remuneration according to the socialist principle of 'from each according to his ability, to each according to his work', all found their expression in the new Economic Management and Planning System (SDPE).

Largely resembling the post-1965 Soviet planning reform, the system was set up in the framework of Cuba's first two formal five-year plans of 1976-80 and 1981-6. It attempted to put enterprises on a self-financing basis, introduce criteria of profitability and material incentives, and achieve organisational coherence and efficiency. Drawing on a notion of 'centralised pluralism' it in practice increased the level of central consultation with regions, sectors and productive units but continued to be flawed by bureaucracy, irrational pricing and the weakness of financially based incentives in a shortage-type

---

Policy changes in other areas can similarly be traced back to often heated debates throughout 1986-7 in all parts of the island. A July 1986 meeting in Sancti Spiritus province attacked the spurious nature of investment priorities, with an excess of projects started, poor project completion since each part was handled by different enterprises, and hence increasing amounts of outlay on diminishing returns. After much analysis, any new project investment was subsequently cut to a minimum, and emphasis shifted to completing those projects already under way, reorganising them under one enterprise responsible from start to finish.

Another major point to come out of that Sancti Spiritus meeting

---

economy. Between 1976 and 1980, successive innovations were introduced to allow for greater decentralisation and local initiative. Yet there was growing unease as to how these were being worked out in practice, sectorial demands and tensions, and general concern over the lack of integral planning. These demands could arguably be met more easily because of favourable external trading conditions, as could growing material incentives also be met. What was perceived to be a lack of global planning vision, failing to attach importance to and stimulate key non-profit-making sectors and misjudging the constraints of a changing world economic situation, encouraged the political leadership to step in again in 1984 and demand a revamped 1985 plan more in tune with the times.

Two less acknowledged elements in the mid-1980s crisis of 'economic mechanisms' are what might be termed the war economy and the solidarity economy, which are to a certain extent interrelated. The first entails prioritising planning for the national defence effort in times of renewed, strong political hostility from the US and for the war effort abroad, whether in the form of troop involvement as in Angola or military advisers in Nicaragua. The second involves commitments abroad, whereby, just as Cuba has been the recipient of new trading and aid agreements from the socialist camp, so similar arrangements are operated by Cuba *vis-a-vis* needier Third World nations. These range from sugar technology to military, health and education assistance, none of which can operate on a criterion of profitability. It should be clear that these activities are not solely motivated by altruistic considerations. They form part of a project for a safer and sounder world for the smaller peoples of the currently disadvantaged two-thirds of humankind who can hardly hope to prosper alone. To this extent, they inevitably work in Cuba's own long-term interests.

was made by the youth secretary of the sugar construction and assembly enterprise, who was particularly outspoken on the high turnover of management. Her concern was not only the discontinuity that this created in itself, but also that not one of the people appointed had been competent in the post. Jobs had gone through personal channels to outsiders when there were often good younger people on the books who should have been given a chance. Youth promotion is now being assessed much more carefully. In defence of the managers, it was also concluded that the sheer weight of paperwork demanded under the central management system was such as to render administration ineffective. The whole economy was top-heavy with bureaucracy and yet still without effective controls. If enterprises were profitable, they may well have been so at the expense of other areas of the economy and society, and quite often output in quantity was achieved at the expense of quality.

A third point, less popular with some, was raised by the provincial Ministry of Labour secretary who supplied figures, according to which over one third of the province's workers surpassed production targets by 30 per cent. When broken down by sector, this reached 68 per cent in heavy industry, 70 per cent in communications and 72 per cent in construction. In financial terms, over-production accounted for 77 per cent of the province's increased expenditure on salaries and put a strain not only on profit margins of enterprises, but also state finances. Production targets were too low, he argued, if they could be so easily surpassed. Similar arguments were levelled against paying the established 70 per cent of wages to workers temporarily laid off due to factory breakdowns, stoppages, and the like, without rechanneling work effort into other needy areas. And there was opposition to the party secretary of the school bus enterprise, who voiced drivers' demands for round-the-clock (as opposed to the already stipulated 16-hour-a-day) payment during school outings. Doctors, nurses, teachers, and internationalist workers, it was counter-argued, might all be on call 24 hours of the day but do not get paid to the minute.

The issue of wages was to become a central topic of discussion. A month later, a Camagüey industrial construction union leader described his enterprise as the worst in the province, making a loss of eight million pesos in 1985, in part due to excessive wages. Low targets and high bonus and benefit schemes were giving workers 800 to 1,000 pesos a month, as against a national monthly average of around 180. His point was taken up by an industrial engineering union leader who quoted some average monthly wages of over 600 pesos in his sector, rising as high as 1,400 pesos in certain months.

It might seem curious that union leaders should be speaking against, rather than for, higher take-home wages. However, when seen in the wider context, while high rates of extra pay might be to the direct advantage of the workers concerned, they become indirectly detrimental to other workers, who are correspondingly more dependent on the social wage coming out of state resources. It is now the case that the *per capita* social wage, taken to include not only social security but also social consumption (which comprises state-subsidised health, education, transport and communications services, cultural and recreational facilities, canteens, foodstuffs and certain other consumer items) is estimated to be greater than the *per capita* monetary wage. Since no part of the monetary wage is subtracted as national insurance or tax, the financing of the social wage comes entirely out of production. As a consequence, the concept of the social wage, tied in with production, is one that is important to the labour movement and crucial to understanding worker politics in Cuba today.

Services which are provided free of charge clearly involve large sums. In 1987, it was calculated that the average *per capita* cost of education was 160 pesos a month, and for health the figure was 79 pesos. (This might be compared with 11 and 3.5 pesos, respectively, for 1958, though it should be noted that the country then had four million fewer people.) State subsidies on articles considered to be prime necessities were calculated to be in the region of 352 million pesos in state budget figures for 1987. Such social expenditure is one of the main contributing factors to Cuba's population having an average daily nutritional intake far higher than would otherwise be the case for one of the world's less advanced economies, a doctor to every 400 inhabitants, a dentist for every 1,800, a life expectancy of 74 years and an infant mortality rate of 13:1,000, comparable only to the developed industrialised West.

The crux of Cuba's problems today lies precisely in having succeeded in transforming an economy which was run extremely profitably for some at the social, and ultimately political, cost of a vast reserve of casual and migrant labour, chronic unemployment and destitution (with such deficient food and sanitation levels and lack of basic provisions and services as to create endemic parasitism and disease). This transformation has created another economy in which there is such socio-economic security for labour (it is almost impossible to be sacked from a job in Cuba) that the threat of unemployment does not act as an incentive to production, while, at the same time, it is popularly expected that consumer levels will be guaranteed by the government. Cheap labour and the political use

51

of redundancy do not feature in the Cuban context, and are certainly no option in any of its current development drives. The future is defined primarily in terms of higher standards of living for all, and the only way that these can be attained is by increasing output through greater productivity, efficiency and profitability by and for labour. This is what rectification purports to seek, and labour, it is argued, has as much of a vested interest in this aim as any other sector in society.

Politics versus Economics

If there was one constant theme to come out of the sessions building up to rectification, it was that of the social and political ramifications of economic deficiencies. The benefactor, or paternalist state as it has been called in Cuba, with its sense of security and well-being, had led people to take many things for granted and from there to act with indifference or even impunity. 'A kind of day-to-day living without a concern for the future' or 'a centralised sitting back' was how it was described in the 1986 popular press. The need was defined as one of recharging that sense of responsibility for one's actions and those of others, of renewing that ethos of individual and collective care and concern.

There is no easy answer as to what replaces the carrot and stick of capitalist economies. Cuba, like most other socialist countries, has tried different methods at different times. The relative boom years of the late 1970s and early 1980s allowed sufficient leeway for more material incentives, which was the policy of the day under the new economic management and planning system. This was particularly the case where monetary pay was concerned, but also applied to the greater availability of certain goods and services. The leaner years of the preceding period had really invalidated this as an option. There was little in the shops, so there was little on which to spend money earned. This was one of the reasons why so little importance came to be attached to money in the late 1960s and why some could almost literally paper their walls with it. The lack of goods and services was one of the greatest disincentives to labour. It was offset largely by post- revolutionary euphoria and approximations to Che's theory of the New Man, involving mass mobilisations of volunteer labour, though not always in the most productive of ways. Less decorous attempts to mobilise the more disaffected of that early period included the highly unpopular UMAP (Military Units for Production) and the anti-vagrancy law of the mid-to-late 1960s.

The mid-to-late 1980s have in turn created a new dilemma: worker motivation in a new phase of lean years, when a modicum of comfort and the good life has been attained. Crudely put, this means a popular preoccupation with consumer needs at a time when not only can they be less readily met, but when whole areas of consumer goods have never been treated as a priority. A Havana youth, eyeing home-produced and dollar-imported consumer goods in special stores, might mutter in disgruntled fashion that the government does not believe in consumerism for the people, and with an element of truth. While it is the case that the country is nowhere near economically capable of creating an abundance of consumer items, there has at the same time been a tendency to confuse consumption, seen as satisfying increasingly diverse and complex needs, with wanton, luxury consumerism. Cuba is too near the US, and Havana is too young to forget its past as a consumer-mecca. Good clothes, television sets and cars are desirable parts of life. And if acceptable consumer levels are also part of the 'chicken and egg' motivation problem, especially where the metropolis is concerned, it can be argued that future plans will have to take consumerism more and more into consideration. But again, since any increase in import levels is out of the question, the impetus to meeting consumer needs must come from domestic production which will take time to set up, and which presents its own problems.

The eminently political decision to try to stimulate worker motivation by appealing to a higher sense of values, otherwise known as moral incentives, while controversial, has its hard socio-economic rationale. As austerity sets in, the increasing relative lack of material goods can render material incentives counter-productive. With little to buy through legitimate channels, money in circulation acts as a strong inflationary pressure towards dealings in the secondary economy and black market, thereby further undercutting the system for state-subsidised provision. Many of Cuba's workers not linked directly to production that could be normed, such as the vast numbers of health, education and service workers, certainly never had the option of making extra money through prizes, bonuses and the like. They were put at a relative disadvantage to their normed salaried counterparts, with the latters' higher paid contract labour and lucrative street peddling on the side. This created a visible demoralisation and withdrawal of labour in certain areas (including health and education), a more overt absenteeism (figures for the Havana bus company trebled between 1978 and 1986), even backed by sham medical certificates, a general falling off of work productivity, an increase in negligence and therefore work accidents (some fatal, some unintentional, although the Havana international telephone service was totally interrupted in late 1988 through a fire said to have been caused by a disgruntled worker). It compounded the existing problem of over-staffing and diversion of resources into more remunerative channels (such as plastic toothbrushes being bought out and turned into bracelets, earrings and other trinkets for street sale). The more this happened, the more the need for a shake-up became evident. The very parameter of profitability had led to a neglect of less profitable items, some of which were much needed in the consumer area, to the point of reimporting goods that had before been manufactured at home. Espresso coffee pots, brought in from Italy, were a case in point.

An express aim of the rectification process was not to rush headlong into any great changes but to analyse each problem in its place. Certainly, a year after campaigning began, little real change seemed to have been effected. The spate of follow-up meetings throughout the island in 1987 highlighted problems of trying to find decorous ways of relieving tired revolutionaries from posts for which they were no longer, if ever, competent; of tightening up on finance, quality controls and norms; of creating a viable and responsive management and work ethic; and of filling production, distribution and service gaps left by closing down private channels, to mention some of the most salient. Solutions were proving highly elusive. Vested interests had been created and were not about to be easily removed.

In Ciego de Avila, over 20,000 work days were calculated to have been lost between January and March. 'We still get to offices and find men and women talking about the soap opera on television the night before rather than working,' one party member complained. In Santa Clara, there were still enterprises with norms being surpassed by over 30 per cent, and the common complaint was of workers arriving late, leaving early and slipping out on personal errands. One success story was the Santiago de Cuba textile plant, where absenteeism had dropped from 20 per cent in 1986 to 5.6 per cent by mid-1987, output targets were being met for the first time in the plant's history, and, whereas 97 per cent of 1986 textiles had been third class, the first six months of 1987 had registered 11 per cent first class and 58 per cent second. Another was the microbrigade movement. This certainly had a lot to do with the better performance of the Santiago plant, and held for other factories, too. By mid-1987, there were 12,000 men and women in 372 brigades working on a total of 345 buildings, 5,000 apartments, 50 nurseries, ten polyclinics, 12 special needs schools and 600 family doctor home-offices. It must be

---

Straw Hats

Guanabacoa is a strong worker heartland across the harbour from Havana, where the city-dweller would least expect to see peasant farmers in straw hats. Yet in 1988, a whole brigade moved in, exchanging hats for construction helmets, to build one of the many new nurseries for under-sixes in the rectification campaign. Organised by ANAP, the brigade was called Niceto Pérez, after one of the peasant martyrs of the revolution. Individual and cooperative farmer *brigadistas* from all over the country, with peasant and worker back-up from Havana city and province, completed the nursery in a record 80 days, between Peasant and Worker Day celebrations. The name of the nursery symbolised this instance of the peasant-worker alliance: *Sombreritos de Yarey* (straw hats).

---

said, however, that the speed at which the buildings have gone up has not exactly guaranteed high quality finish, and the very scope of construction has put new demands on certain sectors of the economy and workers. An interesting example is the steel industry.

Caribbean Steel

The Antillana de Acero (Caribbean Steel) plant was one that came in for much criticism in the early phase of rectification for its low production targets and high take-home salaries, quoted as 1,000 pesos a month and more. A giant of a rolling mill, it was very much a product — and to a certain extent a showcase — of the revolution.

The factory was set up in 1959, with the nationalisation and merger of Cabilla Cubana (Cuban Rod), Acero Unido (United Steel) and a couple of smaller foundries, functioning on raw materials imported from the US. Most of the country's steel needs were in fact met by imports, and what domestic production there was suffered greatly in the initial years of the revolution with the blockade and exodus of technicians to the US. In the vacuum created, agreements were signed with the USSR to expand and modernise the rolling mills, with Soviet technology and training, largely for the production of corrugated steel and steel bars for reinforcing concrete for domestic construction. Today, the plant has some 5,000 workers and the work is tough. The furnaces and foundry shops are, by modern standards, rudimentary. The noise, heat and dust levels, while monitored for safety, health and hygiene, make heroes out of workers simply for being there. Yet the complex, which functions almost as a town unto itself on the outskirts of Havana, offers comprehensive social facilities. Extensive worker housing has been built in the surrounding area, and the plant has its own polyclinic, polytechnic and social club (complete with swimming pool, restaurant and discotheque), with a nearby school and nursery that the workers also helped to build.

Although there had long been a first-aid post, the polyclinic was completed in 1984. As it stands today, it combines a comprehensive general service and some specialised medical care, along with preventive work medicine. This includes compulsory annual checkups, with a special emphasis on occupational health hazards — accidents and exposure to heat, toxic and other pollution levels, on which the Institute of Work Medicine is constantly checking. Each new investment has to include health and safety measures. Goggles, helmets, boots and gloves are provided for workers in areas where they are considered necessary, though it is fairly common to see workers not bothering to use them. It is the job of a special administrative department, backed by the union, to supervise the area of health and safety. There are factory shortcomings in this regard, it is admitted, but the most common cause of accidents is still worker negligence.

How did rectification affect Antillana? Interestingly enough, the imbalance between salary and production had already been under review at the plant level in October 1985, before the onset of rectification, given that work norms were being surpassed by 15-30 per cent. In 1986, norms were raised, although, since plant production exceeded planned output and was running at a profit, premiums and bonuses were kept for those workers who continued to top the norm. What is called the social stimulation fund, a percentage of profits earmarked for social undertakings, was also left untouched.

The question of norms had to be handled sensitively, 'bearing in mind production, but also the worker', factory trade unionists were quick to stress. Norms were to be 'not too high for a worker to meet, with only profits in mind, but neither geared simply to workers here, but to the people as a whole.' Similarly, a detailed payroll study was made which pointed to some clear overstaffing. Solutions were found in retraining schemes, some of them in the USSR, for expanding parts of the plant; other workers were mobilised temporarily into areas where there was a need for labour (sugar harvesting, for example), on their own factory salary levels, and yet more went into the microbrigade movement.

Microbrigade expansion had a two-fold effect on the plant; firstly, there was the increased demand for the steel rods and other construction components and, secondly, more workers were moved out of production and into construction. While trade union and party waged a strong political campaign on the need for greater worker consciousness, the monetary loss felt by raising norms and the cutbacks on workforce numbers were also offset by the social gains of increased housing and other construction programmes and the wider satisfaction of contributing to the overall construction effort. While this must have been more readily accepted by some than others, the fact of the matter is that, despite occasional production stoppages due to irregularities, such as supplies of imports and lack of coordination, real output has continued to be greater than planned capacity. And the factory has an impressive construction record. Four microbrigades are currently in operation, three comprising workers seconded from the plant, and one made up of retired workers, also organised by the union and building a medical unit. An average of 200 apartments a year are being built in the rather curiously named nearby Berro (Watercress) area of Lotería (Lottery) district. Over 2,000 workers have received apartments over the years through the microbrigade scheme.

There is an observable family tradition within the factory, and this, supplemented by the many training schemes within the enterprise, technical institute and university annex, has guaranteed a steady work force. The greatest turnover is, as one might expect, among the young. Under far from optimal conditions, foundry work continues round the clock on three shifts, and the night shift is far from popular among those under thirty. Special conditions and pay scales for night work have been particular concerns of management, trade union, party and youth.

Antillana today functions as one in a union of five related enterprises, all in the locality. Taking the enterprises as a whole, there are 40 trade union branches, each with a union executive of 11-13 members, for a total of 465 elected representatives. Curiously enough, in such a male bastion of heavy metallurgy, 48 per cent of them are women. The whole technical side of the factory employs women in considerable numbers and women are also very gradually making inroads into jobs that have been traditionally considered to be for men, foundry work included. For them the new nursery was a great achievement, and over one-third of its intake are Antillana workers' children, who perhaps literally live up to the nursery's name: *Obreritos de Acero* (Little Steel Workers).

Cowhide Baseballs

Baseball is Cuba's national sport. It came from the US, of course,

Nursery at Antillana steelworks

Women cigar rollers, La Corona

Handstitching baseballs, INDER

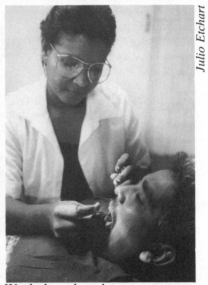

Workplace dental treatment, Antillana

but probably few of the players or fans ever stopped to think twice about it, much less about the fact that that is where the bats, balls and gloves also came from. When they had to, with the blockade, a national sports industry came into being, though not without its difficulties. The efforts that went into producing a Cuban cowhide baseball that would match its US horsehide predecessor mirror similar quests to discover the secrets of what gives soap and toothpaste the right consistency, perfume the right smell and Coca-Cola its fizz, as US multinationals pulled out assets, including trade secrets and technical personnel.

In the case of baseball, all that there had been in Cuba in the first place were small repair shops and representatives of US firms selling bats, balls, gloves and the like. Cut off from its traditional US source, at the very moment of building up a mass sports movement throughout town and countryside, around a sport which could not be catered to by alternate socialist markets (it was hardly their national game), Cuba had to start producing by itself. Machinery began to be installed as early as 1959, and by October 1960 quality baseballs were being turned out. The major change was that these were made of cowhide, not horsehide, because Cuba had no horsebreeding industry to speak of, but did have large numbers of dairy and beef cattle. Substituting the one for the other might seem to some to have been no great achievement, but the hide has to be the right texture, tough but not hard, supple but not stretched, smooth and not marked. The back of the cow, as opposed to the underbelly or neck, is the best. But even today, 30 years on, with sizeable cattle-breeding stations, quality leather supplies are still a problem. The horsehide comes from breeding farms, where horses are not as exposed as open-range cattle to scratches and blemishes from trees, fences and tics. Also, the processing itself had to be different. But it was the beginnings of something big. The balls, with their machine-spun thread inners in hand-sewn leather, are now recognised internationally, and today other parts of the world, the US included, are turning to cowhide rather than horsehide.

The various shoe, bat and glove shops (machinery and workers) were fused with baseballs in 1965, in a factory employing some 200, that developed other small sports lines (chess sets were one), in mostly artisanal fashion. The industry at present boasts a factory in Santiago de Cuba (of about 200 workers), in Florida, Camagüey province (200), Pinar del Río (50), and Havana (1,000), as well as factories producing neon signs, electronic scoring boards, trophies and shoes, all under the umbrella of the National Institute of Sports and Recreation (INDER). The large Havana factory is the most diversified of all, making metal bars and wooden posts (for boxing, gymnastics, basketball and volleyball) and small boats (for rowing and canoeing). By way of example, gloves produced in the Havana, Florida and Santiago de Cuba factories now cover 70 per cent of national needs, and the Havana complex handles 50 per cent of clothing, shoes and balls. Imports from socialist countries go to supply the sports schools and teams, with some minimal imports from the capitalist area for international contests, while national production supplies the mass sports movement. Some 18 per cent of supplies (leather, rubber, resin, plastic, thread and glue) to the Havana factory come from capitalist countries, some 50 per cent are of national production (though perhaps with some external component), and the rest comes from the socialist bloc. Of a current total value of approximately 12 million pesos, one million corresponds to exports, largely to Eastern European and African countries, Nicaragua, and certain capitalist markets.

Again, as in Antillana, conditions are far from optimal. Health hazards include working the hair from the hide, which is then used for glove filling and arrives at the factory complete with earth, insects and other extraneous matter, and which cooling fans can blow through the workshop. Hand-sewing of the balls is done largely by women, with needles in both hands, pulling the thread up and out, and can harm the breasts if not done correctly. Many of the seats are uncomfortable, and lighting in some parts is inadequate. Yet the union has just successfully lobbied for its own gymnasium, sauna and video room, has four buses for worker excursions, and coordinates with the youth section the use of ten bicycles for weekend cycling trips.

Since 1983, a special youth apprenticeship programme has been taken on by the factory, for 14 to 17 year-old secondary school drop-outs, often from problem homes in the surrounding area, and frequently with a record of delinquency. Technically speaking, 17 is the school-leaving age, but these programmes provide an apprenticeship at the factory on reduced hours and a stipend, in return for which the youths are given every encouragement to continue their schooling on an evening or work-release basis. Management, union, party and youth education officers often have to double as social workers, encouraging the young either to stay on or to train in other areas.

A positive side to rectification in the case of this factory has been a strengthening of such social aspects as youth and recreational work, helping to offset readjustments in salaries and norms. Any relocation of staff has been carried out within the factory, as far as possible on the same skill and salary level but never with a demotion of more than two categories, or into the microbrigade movement. The factory has two microbrigades of its own, and contributes workers to other brigades in the area, as well as to agriculture when needed. Stoppages, usually partial, that is of one production line or another, have largely been due to irregularities in supplies, no doubt in part due to administrative incompetence, but much more to currency restrictions on foreign imports and production and distribution bottlenecks in internal supplies. The ability to channel workers affected into other productive areas has helped economic viability and has been crucial to overall morale, even if creating its occasional point of irritation.

La Corona Cigars

La Corona cigar factory is, in many ways, the antithesis of the sports factory. Dating back to the l9th century, it testifies to a whole historical process. La Corona was set up in 1845 with German capital and grew steadily, catering to first European, and then US markets for luxury cigars. By the turn of the century, it was one of the big Havana export factories to fall into American Tobacco Company (ATC) hands, as did 90 per cent of the Havana cigar export industry. The current factory site (where the Villanueva Theatre had once stood, before being first closed and then burned down in the early passions of Cuba's 1868-78 First War of Independence against Spain, an episode proudly recorded in La Corona history) was where all ATC export cigar production was gradually concentrated, as factories were merged, and output and work force cut back. The reasons for this lay in the transfer of manufacturing to the US, with quality imported leaf from Cuba, to beat tariff and other protectionist barriers. When, in l932, at the height of the Depression and in the wake of one of the biggest strikes to shake the Cuban tobacco industry, ATC transferred Havana production to a holding company, Tabacalera Cubana, SA, the sizeable US market had already gone and it was to domestic and mainly smaller Latin American markets that Havana hand-rolling was directed.

A workforce that had once exceeded 5,000, now stood at a mere 250. What had been Cuba's l9th-century labour aristocracy had been much beaten down, and its militancy undermined. Nonetheless, La Corona stood as a symbol of foreign domination, much as its workers and their leaders epitomised opposition to it. They had waged many a battle, including keeping machine production out, and stood among the forefront of Cuba's communist-led trade union movement of the late 1930s and 1940s, so much so that in the 1946-7 US-spearheaded anti-communist purge of Cuban unions, La Corona worker and union activist, Miguel Fernández Roig, was shot dead in a factory occupation by hired gunmen. Many of Cuba's nationalised factories of the 1960s were renamed after martyrs, and it was only logical that this one should have been named after Fernández Roig. It has subsequently seen more mergers with other former large-scale enterprises, for instance Por Larrañaga, the factory from which emerged Carlos Rodríguez Carreaga, Fernández Roig's successor in the Havana cigar makers' union and also in death (he too was shot, in 1958).

Walking into La Corona factory today is something of a poignant journey into the past. The splendour and elegance of old have gone with the ravages of time, blockade and blight. With production and workforce depleted in the 1960s, the quality of its cigars did not go unaffected, and, although the tobacco recuperation of the 1970s helped to restore traditional standards, blue mould was a tremendous setback in the harvest of 1980-81. Nonetheless, the much improved agricultural extension work enabled tobacco growing to recover quickly, and, just as farmers were given due compensation, so redundant workers were sent home on 70 per cent pay. This last measure has been revised with rectification, and in the event of factory stoppages now, every attempt is made to find alternative work. Again, the factory has two microbrigades, and a third is planned. Production and export markets (the US excepted) have expanded again recently. The 'Habano', as the generic term came to be known, is still regarded in the trade as the world's greatest luxury cigar, and La Corona factory alone turns out some 24 different kinds. Even so, annual production stands at about 12 million cigars and exports at about nine million, in comparison with the 32 million of the early 1960s.

Talking to militant old cigar makers at La Corona today is a lesson in itself, not only in how past forces have gone to shape Cuba's destiny, but also in how whole sectors of workers have had to adapt to very different, and often less privileged, realities. The same could be said about the white collar workers of Cuba's former General Electric or Bell Telephones companies. Upheaval and blockade, some wise and some not-so-wise policies, have all contributed to this change in fortunes. In tobacco, the process was not helped by a post-revolutionary reaction against tobacco, that took much longer to resolve itself than in the case of sugar. The drastic halving of the crop between 1966 and 1970 was accompanied by overstandardisation of a product whose markets rested on fickle taste, and a depletion

---

Industrialisation

While Cuba was a primarily mono-exporting agricultural country, it was also one of the first in Latin America to have an industrial base and proletariat. There was considerable 19th-century British, German, and French investment, in addition to Spanish colonial interests, and ultimately US capital, such that by the 20th century huge multinational ventures included Havemeyer, Cuban American Sugar, United Fruit, Cuban Cane, American Tobacco, Bethlehem Iron, Cuba Central Railways and Cuba Eastern Railroad, backed by banking capital in the form of the West Indies Finance Corporation and the National City Bank of New York.

Apart from the large numbers of sugar workers on the post-emancipation estates, there were already by the late 19th century considerable factory concentrations of tobacco workers, railway and dock workers, especially in Havana. The 20th century saw the addition of significant numbers of workers in light industries, such as textiles, and soaps and detergents (Colgate-Palmolive). The trend was, however, towards trade and service sectors (Bell Telephone, General Electric).

---

of whatever skilled workforce remained as other areas proved more attractive. One result was the drive of the mid-1960s to train women cigar makers — a move considered little short of scandalous in the context of male-dominated export cigar rolling. There had been women rolling cigars in the home, or at best on an ephemeral basis in small outfits catering strictly to local markets, but this was something quite different. Women in large quantities (in fact outnumbering the men) were the stemmers (taking the central stem out of the leaf before rolling), and in smaller quantities the ringers (putting the cigar band on afterwards), as well as office clerks, cleaners and canteen staff. They were also the packers of cigarettes. Now, master cigar makers were being called upon to train substantial numbers of young women, over periods of six to nine months, when apprenticeships had formerly lasted anything up to four years.

A skilled woman cigar maker of La Corona today remembers those early days:

> I was one of the first to be trained through the Federation of Cuban Women. I thought I'd like it. I'd heard a lot about tobacco, and what the factories were like, and that they were looking for women. The first few days were really something, but then we began to get the hang of it. After the course, we were sent out to the various factories. It was

63

difficult at first with the men, not having the experience, but we all gradually got used to it and each other. It's easier for the newer generations of women coming in, because they each sit next to someone who works with them, whereas we had one instructor for the whole class.

Another woman recalls: 'When I started, I couldn't see anything in it and was bored. But then I began to like producing something with my own hands, I felt motivated.' The gender change has been so great over the last 20-odd years that cigar making is fast coming to be seen as a woman's trade. The women, like the men before them, progress from the smaller, easier cigars ('Entreacto', for instance) to the majestic 'Gran Corona'. What is different is that since 1969-70, the old piece-rate, by the thousand, according to the kind of cigar being made, has been changed to a work norm system. Master rollers on top cigars were used to good rates of pay and no set hours. In their hey-day they were famed for having money to throw away on gambling, drink and women as the mood took them. Those who are still in the industry today have what is called a 'historical wage' (which has been deliberately kept at the high pre-revolutionary rate in keeping with the policy to upgrade, but never downgrade, salaries) and are inclined more to work than to dissipation. For example, La Corona has its cigar maker who is also a National Hero of Labour cane-cutter; he produces the 'Gran Corona' and is paid 307 pesos for the norm, on the basis of the historical wage, as against the stipulated 217 pesos.

For the rest, according to the kind of cigar, a work norm is set for the eight-hour day, and anything produced over and above the norm is paid extra. Good cigar makers, men and women alike (for whom pay scales are identical), can still make more than the norm and earn good take-home pay, albeit not so high as that of their elders. As elsewhere in the country, norms are monitored, and if the majority of workers are meeting them by more than 30 per cent, or falling short of meeting them by over five per cent, then they are revised. Norms in the tobacco industry are currently up for revision, but it is a sensitive area, especially as production needs to be boosted. Cuba is not meeting hard-currency market demand, and clearly does not want any disincentive to production because of lower pay scales. As the union secretary for work organisation and wages put it: 'I have to be on my toes when a revision comes up so that no error of judgment is made regarding a given group of workers'. Going on to talk about the changing role of the unions, he expressed this as a need to:

reconcile our interests as the working class with those of our revolutionary state. Our main role is as a harmonious, not antagonistic, counterpart to management. The union's role is to represent and defend the interests of the workers who elect us. That includes the quality of our product, because on that depends the ethics of our state, our people and our working class.

Before taking this up in a wider context, it should perhaps be said that the strong political tradition of a group like the cigarmakers has traditionally been accompanied by an emphasis on education and culture. The factory reader is a tradition that is still maintained, as workers have read to them an hour of news and an hour of a novel each day. The only difference is that, whereas the reader's salary used to come out of the pockets of the workers, it is now part of the factory payroll. The novel being read at La Corona in the summer of 1988, by popular demand, was a Cuban edition of an Italian melodrama entitled *Bridge of Sighs*. The cultural secretary of the union is a young woman, whose job ranges from hiring dance groups, organising informal talks with artists, writers and performers, coordinating the factory's lively cultural movement (singers, poets, etc) to arranging sports and recreational activities such as dominoes, table tennis, chess and day trips to Varadero beach resort.

The Role of the Unions

To bring together some of the points raised by the different experiences of the Antillana, INDER and La Corona factory workers, it is worth turning to present union policy on wages and work organisation, as expressed in the rectification campaign. But this can hardly be seen out of the context of the changing role of trade unions during these three decades of revolution. Most important is that, while the party has a membership of about half a million and the youth organisation another half million, the Central Organisation of Cuban Trade Unions (CTC) groups together 3.3 million workers. This necessarily means that it is a force to be reckoned with. The exact role it has to play, however, has been as much a controversial issue in revolutionary Cuba as in all socialist revolutions.

There were workers involved in all stages of the insurrection, from the 1953 attack on the Moncada Garrison, through the expedition from Mexico to Cuba aboard the *Granma* to the rebel army in the mountains and underground movements in the cities. It can also be argued that the January 1959 general strike was crucial to consolidating the rebel forces' victory. However, none of these actions was carried out by a working class institutionalised through the trade unions. The more militant unions had had their support base cut away in the 1947-8 cold war conflict within the labour movement. This led to some uneasy alliances in the early years of the revolution, with certain sectors of the working class out to defend their own interests, and created a double-sided phenomenon. One argument ran that there was no need for unions in the classless worker-peasant state; that the revolutionary government could legislate for all. Local unions were left rather disjointed, and the CTC was little more than a formal channel for issuing general guidelines. This, it is now conceded, ran counter to the very essence of trade union structure, which must be one of separate, though affiliated organisations that can articulate the necessarily specific concerns of the various sectors of workers. It was impossible to take measures across the board, and the 1970s saw a strengthening of the unions, especially after the 1973 CTC Congress.

It gradually became clearer that under socialism the unions have to play a double role: they must represent the individual and collective interests of their workers, but they must also concern themselves with the economy, since the very standards of living and well-being of workers depend ultimately on economic growth. The problem is that this double role will never be easy. One example of this tension was to be found in the controversial Resolutions 32 and 36, introduced by the Ministry of Labour in the late 1970s. The former placed in abeyance the Workers' Councils, which had hitherto decided on sanctions for more flagrant breaches of labour discipline, and empowered the administration to dismiss a worker after three warnings. The latter was its counterpart, in that it provided for workers taking the administration to court. By the early 1980s, it was clear that 32 was being used much more than 36, and there were vociferous complaints from many sectors of workers that 32 was being abused, sometimes for getting rid of more problematical workers, occasionally for purely personal reasons.

There will always be a latent contradiction between the immediate interests of workers and wider social interests. These have to be harmonised as far as possible, as in wage policy, for example. The current CTC national secretary for wages and work organisation explains:

> There has to be a balance between sectors. You can't have one sector way ahead of another because it happens to be economically more viable or has strong leaders. A union is always going to try for the best where its workers are concerned... At the same time, too much uniformity can be counterproductive. The other problem of all revolutions has been precisely the strong trend toward egalitarianism,

with a more just and more equitable distribution of wealth. There are those who want equal treatment for all cases, without considering that similar work might entail higher risks in one sector than in another, might present greater complexity, and might be in an area where labour is scarce and therefore needs to be doubly attractive. Wage differentials play an important part in channeling labour, from town to countryside, to unattractive but socially necessary work, to night work. But differentials will always be a problem. Workers always want the wages of the best-paid. Nobody says, 'I'm earning too much, pay me less'! The CTC may find itself at one moment consolidating new gains for a given sector, and at others having to explain to those same workers that what they want cannot be.

There are areas where egalitarianism does prevail; health is one, education another, with equal access for all regardless of work. But even then there may be some differentials; Antillana has its polyclinic, for example, because of the high risk factor of foundry work. Within these two sectors, also, problems have arisen. Greater efficiency is being called for within the health service, and at the same time there are demands for better conditions and pay for those lower down the scale, such as cleaners and ancillary staff. It has been recognised, finally, that educational effectiveness cannot be measured by student pass-rates, as this promotes a trend towards lowering grading standards. Scientists and technical personnel each need different treatment. Where production is concerned, payment according to output was rightly seen as crucial, and a massive wage reform of the early 1980s embodied this principle. Where it went wrong was in not monitoring output targets or norms, such that the productivity/wage relation was thrown out of balance. What started as a desire to attract labour into the refinery, nitrogenous fertiliser plant, or refuse collection, ended up with those in other areas earning more. As a result, the wage mechanism has remained the same, with the norms being altered, in certain sectors. In the words of the CTC: 'If we do not achieve a balance between wages and productivity, the country will go to rack and ruin. Money in circulation in excess of products available for consumption will produce an inflation which will bring absenteeism, labour instability and ultimately more difficulties for workers, because there will be both less purchasing power and less to buy.' The problem, as acknowledged, lies in achieving this balance in what some have called one of Cuba's most difficult moments to date in external, as much if not more than internal, terms.

3. Ethics of Liberation

One of the hubs of Havana life is the intersection of 23rd and L Streets, whose four corners are marked by the old Havana Hilton, today Habana Libre, the Coppelia ice cream parlour, the Yara cinema and the 23 y L bookshop. Further up 23rd, away from the sea, stands another landmark: a Henry Moore-sized, Giaconetti-inspired Don Quixote, carved out of metal. Poised on horseback, his lance at the ready, he might well be on the verge of leaving his small park to attack the sails of the next windmill crossing his path.

The statue is more than symbolic. The legendary 16th-century knight created by Spanish writer Miguel Cervantes Saavedra is to those of Spanish descent what King Arthur might be to Anglo-Saxons, representing that same chivalry and romanticism combined in the pursuit of a noble cause. Maybe such a combination is what to a certain extent fires revolution, and Cuba, like Latin America, has throughout its history had many a Quixote figure. The continent had its great early 19th-century Quixotic independence fighters, best symbolised by the Liberator Simón Bolívar, and its many popular *caudillos:* Emiliano Zapata in the 1910 Mexican Revolution, Augusto César Sandino in the Nicaragua of the 1930s. Analogous Cuban figures would be the late 19th-century independence leaders José Martí and Antonio Maceo, Julio Antonio Mella in the 1920s, and Fidel Castro and Camilo Cienfuegos in the 1950s. As social and political movements inspired great leaders, so they also inspired masses of followers, from peasants to workers, beggars to bandits. Ideals transcended national boundaries and drew supporters from near and afar. It was hardly to be expected that the Cuban revolution would be any exception, and the most Quixotic of all was not Cuban but Argentinian: Che Guevara, whose death in Bolivia in 1967 also lent him the qualities of a martyr.

Guevara was much more than a Quixote, but the image is relevant. He was an idealist and a fighter for a better world, one of greater justice, equity and freedom. He trained as a medical doctor but became a guerrilla fighter to redress the causes of the poverty and ill health he saw around him in Latin America. He first met Castro in Mexico and joined the *Granma* expedition to Cuba. After successfully applying the guerrilla *foco* strategy in Cuba's 1950s insurrection, he lent his talents to fighting in the Congo in the early 1960s. When he left for Bolivia in the mid-1960s, he wrote in his farewell letter that the time had come to mount his steed Rocinante (Quixote's horse) and fight the struggle in new pastures.

There was also Guevara the pragmatist and theorist. While he may arguably have achieved fulfillment fighting great causes on the military front, as Cuba's minister of industry and president of the National Bank, he attempted to lay the foundations for industrial and financial policy and travelled extensively seeking closer political and economic ties with socialist and Third World countries. In his critique of political economy, he analysed Lenin's thinking in the 1920s on the viability of a mixed economy in the context of economic mechanisms peculiar to competitive capitalism: market mechanisms which could be used and regulated by the state. In the Latin American neocolonialism of the 1950s and 1960s, he saw these market mechanisms as less relevant than the financial mechanisms of monopoly capitalism, which were what led him to view budgetary finance as the means of state control. The budgetary system in the economic field was to go hand in hand with ideological concerns, with an education and a civil society grounded on moral ethics. Thus, he also wrote on his vision of the making of the New Man in the process of socialist change, motivated by a higher sense of values, by moral as much as material incentives. He spoke a powerful language of individual, socio-economic, national and ultimately international political liberation.

He has been a very much revered, if somewhat polemical figure since. Aside from his Latin American and wider world acclaim, in Cuba his presence has lived on. Moreover, many a change has sought legitimacy in his thinking. That held as much for the introduction of the new economic management and planning system, with its attempt at greater decentralisation and material incentives, in the mid-1970s, as for the ways in which the system is being called into question today, with renewed emphasis on central planning and moral incentives. In the first, Humberto Pérez, the then minister-president of JUCEPLAN, went to great lengths to argue the continuity of thought with Guevara's analysis of the need for the right balance

Laurie Sparham/Network

Young Pioneer: 'We'll grow up like Che'.

between material and moral incentives in socialist construction. With hindsight, it is agreed, Pérez's virtue was to have injected some sense of order into the Cuban economy, his sin that of allowing material incentive (plus, it might be said, foreign debt and the import mentality) to get out of hand. At least, that would seem to be the reason for his fall from grace when the rectification process began. As the pendulum has swung in the opposite direction, historical coincidence has been in its favour; the 20th anniversary of Guevara's death in October 1987 and the 60th anniversary of his birth in June 1988 were occasions to review Guevara's thinking and to appeal anew to people's sense of altruism and commitment.

Is such an appeal in the 1980s doomed to fall on deaf ears? Or does Cuba have its new social critics and dreamers? This chapter argues that it does, from some predictable, but also from some unforeseen, quarters.

Liberation Theology

The professed ideology of the Cuban state and party might be firmly atheist, yet there are widely held and arguably growing religious beliefs in the society at large. The last ten years have witnessed something of a revival of both the Catholic and Protestant Churches, and a certain strengthening of beliefs behind the more popular syncretic religious forms, a fusion of African and Christian religions. There have always been exceptions to the atheist rule; with her strong Catholic views, Celia Sánchez, one of the leading women fighters in the insurrection, close to the centre of state power until her death several years ago, was one of the better known. And if there has been no attempt by government to emphasise Cuba's radical religious heritage, neither is it exactly taboo. The judicious silence could rather be attributed to uneasy Church-state relations. As these have been ironed out, in a process of mutual consensus the Church-state dialogue has reached a point at which it would hardly be prudent for the state not to accommodate religious beliefs, and, it has been suggested, even the party has members who practice their religions, especially of the syncretic kind. *Santería*, *Abakua* and other cults have traditionally been strong in popular districts or *barrios*, and from the beginning of the revolution until today it has been common to find, in the humblest of households, statues of the Virgin Mary (more likely the syncretic Santa Bárbara), alongside glasses of water for the spirits and pictures of Fidel, Camilo and Che. It was only to be expected that this would be carried over into party and state structures as these reflected their wider grass-roots base among the people.

The origins of the three main religious currents — Catholicism, syncretism and Protestantism — can be traced to particular periods and facets of the island's historical development: Spanish colonialism, black African slavery and US neocolonial domination. Identified first with Spanish colonial rule and then with the more conservative 20th-century oligarchy, Catholicism continued to be the official religion up until the time of the revolution. However, particularly with the successive US military occupations of 1898-1902 and 1906-8, Protestant denominations were established by US settlers associated with large and smaller-scale industrial and finance capital. Each tended to cater more to the middle and upper classes, while the mass of the poorer, largely non-Church-going people developed a fusion of quasi-religious, quasi-mystic beliefs that coloured daily life in the form of spiritualism, *Santería*, *Abakua*, and *Palo Monte*, etc. The sheer force by number and lateness of slave arrivals direct from Africa into Cuba (by the mid-19th century blacks comprised 70 per cent of Cuba's population and abolition did not occur until 1886) meant that, when both a political movement against Spain and a national culture were being forged, the African language and culture were to be extremely influential. This was never altogether reversed, despite the 20th-century change in population balance (60 per cent white by the 1950s) and the attempted Jim Crow-type institutionalised racism (complete with segregated parks and buildings). Still today, *Santería* chants might be sung by whites and blacks, but in the Yoruba language of northern Nigeria.

This singular blend of religiosity was divorced from the Church as an institution. Even so, there was a radical Cuban theology that can be traced back to the turn of the 19th century and the growth of the modern sugar state, with Father Félix Varela. The nascent Cuban bourgeoisie abandoned Christian charity in coming to terms with slavery and the slave trade. Varela voiced the philosophical and religious reaction to their free trade economics. As Cuba's Vice-President Carlos Rafael Rodríguez pointed out, in a reprinted article of 1938 in *Granma Weekly Review*, this idealist criticised submission to the Gospel and the Church fathers. 'Credulity', Varela declared, 'is the patrimony of the ignorant; methodical doubt is the domain of the wise. Experience and reason are the only rules of knowledge...The people have a certain sense that is seldom mistaken, and so it is best to always start by believing or at least by suspecting that they are right.' Varela was blamed by Spain for the beginnings of Cuba's rebellion and he certainly defended a separatism that could be seen as a forerunner to independence struggles.

More modern-day successors in the radical Catholic tradition were Father Guillermo Sardinas, who rose to the rank of *comandante* in the 1950s Rebel Army, and student martyr José Antonio Echeverría, killed covering a pirate radio broadcast for a free Cuba that was meant to coincide with an aborted attack on the Presidential Palace in 1956. Motivated more by social than theological concerns, they were but two of many religious people involved in the struggle against Batista. Their story is being documented by former Radical Catholic Action militant Raúl Gómez Treto, under the auspices of the Latin American Church Commission/Cuba. Treto has also taken a sober look at the Catholic Church (and its initial self-assumed role of 'nobility' facing the 'rabble') in the various phases of Church-state relations during the period of socialist construction. The first, from 1959-60, he describes as one of 'disconcertion', as, in this anti-imperialist, popular democratic phase of the revolution, the Church hierarchy tried to use its influence against any radicalisation of society toward communism, and in its failure became 'disconcerted'. The second, from 1960-63, was one of 'confrontation', as the clergy attempted to pit believers against the revolution and in the process lost many followers. The Church became more and marginalised, and some of the clergy were expelled for counter-revolutionary activity. The third phase, one of 'evasion', from 1963-7, saw an exodus of many remaining believers, a migratory wave which emptied the churches even further.

The year 1968, a turning point for the Latin American Catholic Church in general with the growing social thinking embodied at Medellín, marked a 're-encounter', as the Catholic bishops called for an end to the imperialist blockade of Cuba and for Catholics in Cuba to join in the work effort. This phase lasted until 1979, the year of Puebla, when the present period of 'dialogue' began. Since then, the Church has recognised the significant advances that have taken place in Cuban society and, in international matters, has agreed with the government's unequivocal position on the immorality of the foreign debt and the need for a new international economic order.

When Protestant US missionaries began their evangelising work, they did so very much against the established Catholic Church. However, their Gospel was also closed and conservative; eternal salvation was to be sought through individual piety. Their strict morality went hand in hand with an excessive credulity, or lack of interest in political and economic affairs, and they certainly never questioned their own country's political role in the area. The

The New Evangelism

'The Cuban Church is rediscovering new forms of evangelism. The main thrust of the Cuban Church's evangelising work before 1959 was charity work: church schools, hospitals, homes for the elderly and other institutions serving society. The dynamic of Cuban society caused us to take up new challenges in a socialist society which coincides with the Gospel in its defence of ethical values.

The Church as an ecclesiastical structure has tended to shy away from taking any clear, prophetic stand on societal issues. The contradiction is that the Church, both Protestant and Catholic, has within it members who are in places of work and study, who are members of the Committees for the Defence of the Revolution, of the Federation of Cuban Women, and who have a constructive position in society. But then on entering church what we call the dichotomy, the dualism of faith, begins. Everything changes, and the Gospel is not received in such a way as to convey the message of Jesus Christ in the context of building something new...

The revolution has motivated my faith on more than one occasion. In my personal life, I have lived crises of faith, crises that have stemmed from incomprehension of the Church and its incomprehension of the struggles of society. I am by no means enamoured of pain, but the revolutionary process has stimulated me, as it has stimulated other young Christians to play a conscious part in it. This implies strengthening one's Christian identity in a society that calls itself Marxist, socialist, atheist... Daily practice in Cuban society has inspired me to understand that theoretical atheism is not as important as practical atheism, and that at times religious people can be atheist in practice. We preach what we don't practice, we defend what we don't practice...

Our churches have their religious fanatics who shy away from any political or social dimension. We need to evangelise from a different perspective, from that of helping build the new society. Maybe our motivations are different, but I don't think so. The best values in human beings, men and women alike, must be reaffirmed. There are facets to be strengthened such as the liberation of women, problems to be discussed such as homosexuality and prostitution, not that these are major social problems in Cuba, but the Church needs to face up to them. What is it that makes certain of our youth go off the rails, when they have everything, free schooling, health care, opportunities for cultural and academic betterment? The Church does not have the absolute right but should discover where the possibilities lie for strengthening the construction of a new society.'

Father Angel Ortíz (25-year-old black United Reform Church Minister from Matanzas), August 1988 revolution and the deterioration in US-Cuban relations caused many to leave. For the Cuban Protestants left behind, it represented a turning point in reinterpreting their economic and also spiritual dependence on US mother churches. Their beliefs were those of a sub-culture, cut off from its source, and with few roots among the people. Little by little, however, they have come to reevaluate those positive values of their faith they feel can be revitalised in a revolutionary process like that of Cuba: values such as vocation and liberation from sin in the quest for a new kingdom on earth. 'Our faith is deeply spiritual. In a society like ours, the spiritual acquires great meaning. It is not only economics which determines social action; there are other subjective, spiritual stimuli', it was said by way of summary at a meeting in the Theological Seminary of Matanzas in 1984 on 'The Missionary Heritage of Cuban Churches'.

The importance of that meeting was two-fold. In the first place, it brought together the more progressive elements in the US mother churches with their Cuban counterparts, to agree on three new premises for ecumenical work: the importance of dialogue between the Churches in times of great tension between the two governments; the recognition that there are no longer those who give and those who receive in missionary work, but that there is rather a new mission in which all can give and receive; and that the most valuable missionary work, given the political tensions between Cuba and the US, lies in the struggle for peace and justice. Secondly, it provided a forum for evaluating varied aspects of ecumenical endeavour in the new Cuba, from liturgy and theology to the social and cultural failings of preaching that has not sufficiently challenged the emphasis on individual rather than collective salvation, or evaluated the role of blacks, women and minority groups such as homosexuals in the Church, or explored more popular cultural roots linked with Afro-Cuban religious forms. In addition to their rereading of the Bible, participation in voluntary work, and contribution to national and international forums, more forward-looking Churches are conducting services set to a *salsa* equivalent of Gospel singing.

Historically speaking, in times of great change and upheaval, religion can exert a massive appeal. Catholicism and Protestantism hardly have that appeal in Cuba today, but perceive themselves as a growing voice, filling perhaps a more spiritual void in the national conscience, in tune with the growing Catholic liberation theology and Protestant 'God's option for the poor' in the Caribbean and Latin American area. The mass appeal is arguably still in that more nebulous spiritual and Afro-Cuban religiosity, which is as much a set of cultural values and attitudes to life as a theology.

Cultural Liberation

In the racial and cultural diversity out of which Cuba has grown, the politics of a wider cultural liberation are inevitably liable to be complex and, it might be argued, at the best of times fraught. It is one of the miracles of the revolution that political unity created a sense of cultural unity, although there are times when that unity has been stretched. The original maxim of the fledgling revolution — 'within the revolution everything, against it nothing' — was an attempt at containing diversity on the basis of set political parameters, at the time defined broadly enough to embrace all that mattered. It encapsulated the popular rejection of elite, anti-revolutionary values. The problem, as time passed, is that it ran the danger of being one of those catch-all phrases, wielded indiscriminately by the powers that be. In some of its worst moments, it degenerated into what was boldly described in 1988 as the 'cultural terrorism' of the late 1960s and early 1970s. This ranged from prohibition of the Beatles and long hair as degenerate Western culture and of a growing black cultural movement as black separatism, to the *cause célèbre* of writer Heberto Padilla's conflict with the authorities. Prohibition, of course, always arouses interest, and it is to one of the literary outlaws of those times that many of the young writers of the 1980s look: the late Catholic writer José Lezama Lima, who embraced the revolution and its promise of a new Cuban intellect, but on his own terms. It is not so much his Catholicism but his philosophical and literary complexity that appeals to those who are the products of an essentially lay education, and much more so where simple political formulas have often proved inadequate.

Lezama Lima, who was from a white educated background, took second place to Cuba's newly declared National Poet, the communist mulatto Nicolás Guillén. The racial reference here is quite deliberate, for Guillén represented the Martí dictum of the 'not black, not white, Cuban'. He symbolised the race redeemed, in the free republic envisaged by Maceo and other 19th-century forebears, Domingo Aponte and Guillermón Moncada, by the 20th-century black working-class leaders, the dockers' Aracelio Iglesias, tobacco's Lázaro Pena and sugar's Jesús Menéndez. His poetry was eminently political and rhythmic, easy to understand and easily set to music. But the redemption of which he spoke proved to be more elusive; racial discrimination can be addressed but racial prejudice runs deep.

While Guillén's poetry was a positive affirmation, a lesser known black historian of those years, Walterio Carbonell, a university student from Castro's days, and like him from a landed family, was seen as more negative. In the revolutionary renewal, he wanted faster recognition for the contribution blacks had made to their country's history and culture, and greater integration at all levels of the national effort. In the interests of unity, his and other similar calls of the 1960s were judged to be potentially divisive. It was not until a decade later that they were taken up by party and government, paving the way for more serious analyses of the contemporary black question and, in the mid-1980s, the first steps towards positive monitoring of equal opportunities policies. On one level, blacks and Afro-Cuban cultural forms have never had such official recognition and support, as in the National Folklore Group and the African and Caribbean Studies Centres. And yet underlying tensions surface in new ways. There are still fewer black writers than musicians. A non-white who criticises the lack of black faces in the media, let alone government circles, will elicit a white's jibe that blacks have already taken over sports and music. Meanwhile, it is symbolic that a continuing polarisation of cultural preferences has kept rock music on the television, while reggae is confined to street cassettes.

In many other ways, there is evidence of new philosophical debates thirty years on. With well over half the current population born within that time span, concerns are bound to evolve, born of the successes but also the shortcomings of the revolution. A good gauge of this is the country's music, which has traditionally had a strong element of social comment mixed with dance music and love songs, whether from the old troubadour-style singers, and their successor, the now 20-year-old New Song Movement (*Nueva Trova*), or the biting *guarache*, *charanga* or *guaguanco*. The Cuban *Nueva Trova* emerged as part of a wider Latin American political protest song movement reflecting the larger convulsions of the continent in musical form. It was also uncompromising in its treatment of national issues. In 1967, Silvio Rodríguez was taking a risk by singing 'I have to live, I have to speak / I have to say what I think'. Already a star, he was no less intransigent in 1980: 'I owe a lot to the new / truth, joy and adventure / but I get sick with fury / when I'm told what to do /With heads of old iron / and opportunists I've a duel / yet with love and fire / I'll wade through the mire'. The equally popular Pablo Milanés' rejoinder came with song titles such as 'I love this island' and 'I'm staying' (both composed not long after the Mariel exodus); but 'I don't live in a perfect society/ I beg you, don't call it that,' caused some controversy in the early 1980s. At the same time, popular bands were producing more mundane but equally socially significant lines: from 'Saltfish 'n bread' (when there was little else to be had in the late 1960s) to 'Architect of space' (referring to loft-building in tenements as a popular response to the housing shortage of the 1980s) and 'Havana's busting at the seams' (a parody of a crowded city). The contentious 'Nobody loves nobody' of early 1988 was overtaken in the summer by 'Ese hombre está loco' (The man's crazy), seen by some as an irreverent homage to some of Fidel Castro's more ambitious schemes.

One area where the popular social conscience has been less advanced is that of women, as reflected by lines such as 'If she cooks like she moves'. This is only one of a range of dance and love songs, running against the grain of the official promotion of women's liberation. One indication of how such male groups may be falling behind the times, however, might be seen in Cuba's fast-growing divorce rate, with women often divorcing the men. Long past are the days when Cuba merely celebrated its obvious accomplishments in drawing women into social and political life, giving many an economic independence and dignity they had not experienced before. This process has evolved and, at considerable personal cost, those same women are now challenging areas that are not so acceptable to men. With increased social mobility and decreased fertility, traditional extended family relations have been faster in breaking down than their accompanying values. Even under the present-day Aids threat (so far heavily contained in Cuba through massive screenings and epidemiological controls, including sanatoriums for HIV-positive cases), men are not so ready to curb their *macho* promiscuity. 'Titimanía' became the 1987-8 catch phrase (and again *salsa* song title) for what was seen to be a resurging craze of older men taking up with younger women.

The case can be made that the way in which rewards are distributed through the workplace and not the home acts as a major disincentive to men making any significant contribution with the family and home. The ideal worker, not the ideal couple, obtains the rewards. For the woman, this has all too often meant either a reinforcing of traditional roles and domestic submission while the man concentrates on bringing those rewards home, or adding to an already onerous work/home burden by attempting to be exemplary worker, wife and mother. As one extremely active and competent professional woman, four times divorced, put it: 'You end up being an only one-third good worker, wife and mother.' Values, not physical maltreatment or abuse, are the major issues (Cuba has achieved a comparatively non-violent society that spills over into personal relationships). As personal aspirations in relationships lie beyond realities in a society with fewer, but still many, social taboos, obvious trends of the 1980s have been teenage marriages, teenage divorces and single mother families, as women prefer, or have little alternative but to have one less problem: the *macho* man. The social dislocation this creates in terms of stability and affection extends beyond the partners concerned to their offspring and to new generational patterns that include greater rates of juvenile delinquency among the children of 'broken homes'. So far, few argue for a return to the values of old, but many men and a considerable number of women hesitate from pushing things further, while for others such demands are simply not immediate priorities.

This is not to say that committed voices are not making themselves heard. On the contrary, the Federation of Cuban Women and the Feminine Front of the CTC are lobbying hard on this issue, but it has been recognised that change is more complex than might have been thought a decade ago. A noticeable fact is that the more rural the area, the more resistant to change it has been. The introduction of farming cooperatives arguably received greater support from women than men, for good socio-economic reasons. The cooperatives did not necessarily challenge, but actually reinforced, the traditional division of labour as peasant women were relieved to leave field work behind. Today's problems have raised new questions, not only from the FMC, but also within the eminently male bastion of ANAP: is everything being done to help realise women's potential? Within the material constraints, are all avenues explored for providing employment and facilities for women? What are peasant women thinking and doing in this regard? The answers demand concrete grass-roots action from those concerned, as there are today proportionately fewer women in cooperative production and leadership than there were when the movement started. Across the board, women in work are fighting cases of continuing discrimination at the workplace, based on male prejudice rather than any legal premise, and are demanding extended provision to better their condition and position.

The party started the reform process at the 1985 Congress by putting positive recruitment of women high on the agenda and introduced a monitoring system similar to that of blacks, setting quotas on representative party leadership from both groups. The hope is that the example might spread into government and state circles. In the current rectification campaign, aside from the obvious benefits to women and their families in the general boost to home, hospital and school building, one special gain is the renewed priority for building day-care centres. This had not been high on the profit-minded male technocrat's agenda, yet is quite rightly seen by young mothers as crucial to their own continuing advancement and important to a young child's sense of collectivity and sharing.

Women's voices are also emerging in the arts, though with more difficulty. Ironically, three of the four great Cuban films about women's emancipation — *Lucia* (1968), *Portrait of Teresa* (1974) and *Up to a Point* (1983) — were all made by men. The fourth, *In a Certain Way*, (1974) by Sara Gómez, was completed by a male director after her untimely death. This reflects the state of the struggle within the film industry, where, despite substantial numbers of women in behind-the-scenes production, until a special promotion drive over the last couple of years the only women directors were in documentary films. While there are good women poets, women novelists are far fewer today, and the novel as a genre continues to see its women through the eyes of men. More women are to be found among band-members and composers, as opposed to just singers, and now there are more women artists exploring art as a medium for personal as well as societal liberation. This is particularly interesting in the context of the wider young artists' movement that has become embroiled in a debate on the nature of art and society, and the role of the younger generation.

'We cannot be the new Guillén, [writer Alejo] Carpentier or [painter René] Portocarrero. We are the continuing cultural renewal', declared the young artists' Hermanos Saez Association to the 1988 Congress of the Union of Writers and Artists of Cuba (UNEAC). It was at once an affirmation of being in the 1980s and a clamour for recognition in established circles. Only two per cent of participants at the Congress were under 30 years of age. The voice of those who had been born and had grown up during the revolution was therefore not being heard.

The Congress was far from celebratory. It dealt critically with pseudo-cultural folklorist images of Cuba in tourist brochures, sexist images of women selling tropical produce, deficient art criticism and limited information available on cultural developments abroad, while formulating a need for better art education in day-care centres and schools and more cultural promotion at home (including state marketing incentives, credit facilities on the purchase of artistic work, and for overseas cultural representatives directly linked to the cultural world. The verdict of the Congress was that the Cuban people *en masse* have an education, but are not necessarily cultured. 'Massification' has entailed a certain vulgarisation, and out of this a new culture needed to emerge, in which there is a place for 'high culture', but also art education and meaningful community institutions to give people a greater sense of the aesthetic. Hollow institutions on the one hand, and cultural bureaucrats on the other, were seen as major stumbling blocks.

As little as eight years ago, history and philosophy teacher Ariel Hidalgo raised notions of 'the new bureaucratic class' and, ostensibly for proposing the overthrow of that class, ended up in prison on charges of enemy propaganda. The official cultural response (in contrast to that of eight years ago) has been largely one of accommodation to the young artists of 1987-8, who in their writing and art work have attacked institutions, bureaucrats, patriotic symbols and what one of them called 'the late permanence of class antagonisms in socialism'. But many (old and young) feel that these 'angry young men and women' are going too far, are too 'impatient and implacable', and even 'dogmatic', as *Juventud Rebelde* art critic Soledad Cruz put it. The debate has been the interplay between what Minister of Culture Armando Hart called 'that most ancient of contradictions: individual freedom on the one hand, and social discipline on the other'.

Civil and Human Rights

Perhaps where the philosophical debate between the individual and the social, that is, personal realisation in the context of current Cuban socialism, is at its most polemical is in the human rights arena. The Mariel exodus of 1980 was to some a revelation in this respect. Studies carried out since, in Cuba and the US, as to the pushes and pulls of what has been held to be an undeniably political migratory phenomenon have shown overwhelmingly that the exodus cut across all social groupings and that personal considerations and frustrations are what most motivated people to leave. While not all reached the US, this was where most were aiming for, some to join family, many with illusions of the kind of jobs, money, goods and adventure that Cuba could not offer. The limitations they left behind might have been of a socio-economic kind — would-be professionals were looking for new career prospects, homosexuals and blacks hoping for less prejudice, families desiring better housing and the fast food and consumerism of the West, or simply the young finding island confines too constricting. In the eyes of government and the *vox populi*, however, the ones who left became the 'scum','traitors', political escapees. They were repudiated collectively in mass political marches and individually in ugly, if not usually violent, street scenes.

With hindsight, the kind of political statement they were making was really much more about options. These 'boat people' were not driven by hunger or destitution, nor by political repression as might have been suggested. Even the controversial criminals who ended up in Atlanta were not leaving behind unduly harsh prison conditions, as subsequent reports have shown. At their most political, they were more probably making a statement about having fallen foul of the ideologically hard-line, possibly at the local or job level; or they were acting on their perception that the overall regulation of society did not allow for their particular aspirations within the common good.

That few emigres questioned the wider common good testified to Cuba's achievements on this score. And this is where human rights are relevant. For most Western governments, the main focus is on the political and civil rights of the people, concepts that stem from the US Declaration of Rights in 1776 and the 1789 French Revolution and are embodied in the Universal Declaration of Human Rights. This emphasis on civil and political rights all too often precludes collective rights such as those of peoples to self-determination and to disposal of their natural resources. It also precludes those very fundamental economic, social and cultural rights of peoples: at their most basic, the right to eat, the right to work, the right to health, education and housing, in short, the right to life and human dignity. These are the rights that the revolutionary government was aiming to guarantee when it set out to regulate society in such a way as to wipe out hunger, malnutrition, curable diseases, poverty, destitution and illiteracy — and succeeded, creating a society that in its priorities is far more humane, and human, that many of its developing and even developed world counterparts. Just how important they have become to all Cubans was evidenced in the historical irony that Mariel emigres have sharply criticised the extent to which they see these basic values lacking in the US. Conversely, the reopening of family visits in late 1988 to include post-Mariel emigres is a sign of a new flexibility of political principles on the part of the Cuban authorities as regards the Cuba-US migratory phenomenon (which has, it might be said, its own radical roots stretching back into the 19th century). Nonetheless, the humane society having been achieved in Cuba on the macro level, many are now turning to consider political and civil liberties in a new light and are urging further democratisation and a guaranteed place for the dissenting voice.

So far, this has not taken the form of political pluralism as known in the West. There is, of course, nothing to say that democracy is synonymous with a multi-party electoral system. Democracy means government of the *demos*, the majority, and there are many multi-party systems, like the US or the British, that arguably often offer little difference between the major party platforms and legislate less for the majority than for a monied minority. Likewise, there are many Third World capitalist one-party states — Latin America itself has had many — that are not necessarily deemed undemocratic. A socialist one-party state like Cuba can, paradoxically, boast an over 95 per cent turnout for elections in comparison with a 50-60 per cent turnout in the US or Britain. It has also in many ways been able to stimulate more channels of discussion and participation, through community and work organisation, as well as People's Power.

When the National Assembly of People's Power met for the first time in 1976, it ended 16 years in which executive, legislative and judicial powers had been centred exclusively around a tight ministerial cabinet. It came in the wake of a new 1976 Constitution, adopted after a national referendum and embodying many *de facto* changes since the 1959 provisional Fundamental Law and last full Constitution of 1940. In the Latin American tradition of a strong executive, it allowed for a single head of state and government. It also recognised Marxism-Leninism as the state ideology, the Cuban Communist Party (PCC) as the only political party in the country, and relations between the different state organs as based on the principle of democratic centralism. In principle, there are today three institutional pyramids of power: the PCC, the Council of Ministers and the Organs of People's Power, all of which are interlocking. The president of the country is the president of both the Council of Ministers' Executive Committee and the Council of State of the National Assembly of People's Power. Castro was elected to this position for the third consecutive time in 1986, as was his younger brother Raúl, as first vice-president.

There are 169 municipal assemblies of People's Power, functioning as local government bodies, whose delegates are elected by direct secret ballot, according to geographical voting district, for terms of two and a half years. These delegates then elect delegates to 14 provincial assemblies and the 492 deputies to the National Assembly. Their brief covers production and services within their area. At the national level, it is the 'supreme organ of state power' whose functions have included passing yearly and five-yearly plans, the national budget, administrative, civil, penal, public, military and other laws, exercising controls over state and governmental bodies, and appointing members of the Council of State, to serve in between the Assembly's twice-yearly sessions. Since the National Assembly is only in session for a couple of days at a time, the balance of power is tilted in the Council of State's favour. However, although national deputies, like delegates, hold regular jobs and are not paid for their parliamentary functions, they have shown themselves to take their responsibilities seriously and there has been increasing debate about laws and policies. So far, given the integrated nature of the Cuban polity, once policy has become Party policy, endorsed by Castro or other major leader figures, the debate has concentrated more on details than outright opposition. The latter is by no means precluded, but is made highly problematical given that 100 per cent of Council of State members and over 90 per cent of national deputies and provincial delegates are also party members. The figure is lower for municipal deputies (just over 60 per cent), but all figures are substantially higher if Communist Youth membership is also counted.

The role of the party and democratic centralism has always worked better from the top down than from the bottom up. With Castro at the helm for over 30 years, this has had both its virtues and defects. As a leader who has shown himself committed and responsive to his people, he has been instrumental in pushing through great change. As the venerated and all too often undisputed leader, when he makes errors of judgement, the consequences, for party and government, are that much greater. His ability over the years to recognise these consequences and the mistakes made, does not invalidate the need to bolster democratic (in the sense of wider) channels of participation in decision-making. Despite the charismatic strength and direction from a now ageing leader (he was 62 in 1988), the question of eventual succession seems to be less a concern to Cubans than to analysts abroad. The assumption is that Fidel's younger brother, Raúl Castro, will take his place. Nonetheless, what is more on people's minds, arguably as a direct consequence of over a decade of elections and People's Power, are the problems of checks and balances on party and unipersonal government.

Where the decentralisation sought in the 1970s has been more successful is in having placed substantive matters directly related to people's immediate concerns, involving responsibility and decision-making at the local level, in elected delegates' hands. The pothole in the road, the milk arriving late at the shop, the bus stop at a dangerous crossroads, the cigarette factory smoke, the rubbish not being collected: these are the issues at three-monthly public meetings between delegate and electorate. Problems brought up have to be reported back, to the satisfaction of constituents. Hopes raised in the mid-1970s that these kinds of problems could be fixed overnight were quickly dispelled, and a certain disillusionment resulted. People's Power delegates then became a focal point of political education also, finding themselves in the position of having to explain convincingly why there might not be the cement, what the problems were with milk production and distribution. If their explanations were not felt to be satisfactory and they were not seen to be doing their job in representing local interests, the electorate could (and in a number of cases did) withdraw its mandate. Thus, in more ways than one, People's Power became a strong tool for the effective exercise of democracy on local, if not national matters. It might also be argued that the one is an essential prelude to the other, and that increased debate on national affairs today comes of a strengthened sense of political participation and opinion, whether in People's Power or other elective mass organisations such as the CTC, ANAP, FMC and Committees for the Defence of the Revolution (CDRs).

Born as popular vigilante organisations of the revolution, the CDRs developed into a combination of a neighbourhood watch committee and community support group. With over 80 per cent of adult Cubans as members, they undertake a range of activities, from handling blood donations and other health campaigns (like distributing polio vaccine to children), collecting materials for recycling, mobilising for voluntary work in the area, organising evening and night-time watch, and holding meetings to discuss local problems. Their success or otherwise depends very much on the neighbourhood and neighbours concerned, the most common complaint being that of busybody presidents and members of committees. One positive development in 1988 was a resolution prohibiting respective enterprises and agencies from consulting CDRs on job applicants' integrity, precisely so as to avoid the more personal problems among neighbours being used in a wider negative way.

Compared with other revolutions (bourgeois and socialist), Cuba's has been surprisingly open and unrepressive. Far fewer lost their lives, were executed or imprisoned than in, say, the English, French, American or Russian revolutions. Nonetheless, it was to be expected in the 1960s that the revolution would have to close ranks and defend its new existence in the world. Having to do so in the face of military attack, economic blockade, political isolation, and attempts on the lives of its leaders and people meant far from ideal conditions. Revolutionary Tribunals, with a mixture of professional and lay judges, served to contain any spontaneous retribution against 'war criminals'. Their parallel Popular Tribunals, similar in composition, served as a vehicle to mete out justice in the common law field. Each helped establish a contained sense of law and order in a period of great upheaval. In the 1970s, the emphasis was on institutionalisation, that is, consolidating change in institutional forms, including the legal order: hence a new professionalism, the spate of new legislation, and a new court system accountable to the National Assembly. The 1980s have witnessed further reform, to the legislation, criminal and prison procedures, and general judicial thinking.

Deputy Foreign Minister Raúl Roa, who headed Cuba's human rights delegation to Geneva in 1987 and 1988, is one who describes its record as comparatively benign, but makes the point that even today, existence in Cuba:

> 'is not the same as living under more ideal conditions, with no problems of threats, no sinister agencies conspiring to kill, carry out sabotage or introduce sickness and viruses. It has often been literally a question of life or death. The phrase "Patria o Muerte" (Country or Death) meant subsisting, existing, preserving the revolution. This is what lay behind state concern to the effect that anything that could be used to create problems and undermine the revolution was not to be tolerated.'

Cuba, he concedes, has been put on the defensive, although much is changing in the legal and security context. While there are still laws and a whole body of thinking that go back to the early revolutionary period, if not before, significant aspects of this thinking are currently under question, though, as might be expected, not always with a consensus of opinion.

The early-1980s campaign towards prison improvements and the mid-1980s debates on 'social danger' (a precriminal category, allowing the state to hold individuals in custody without criminal charges) and 'enemy propaganda' were witness to such rethinking, as are recurrent arguments on the questions of illegal exit and freedom of association. This last debate is, for the time being, largely confined to small human rights groupings, many of whose members see their organisations as a means towards emigration. Even the political prisoners, of whom Cuba admits there were thousands back in the l960s (1,200 alone from the Playa Girón invasion attempt, and all the rest from some 300 CIA-sponsored counter-revolutionary organisations, internal sabotage and strife), have virtually all gone. More to the concern of the ordinary Cuban citizen is the common criminal, who forms the vast bulk of the prison population and on whom state leniency has now come to rest.

In 1987, giving an overview of the changing spectrum of common crime since the revolution — from what was once murder, assault, drug trafficking, gambling, prostitution and grand larceny to what is now mainly petty thieving, Deputy Minister of Justice Carlos Amat Fores explained how in the l960s 'heavy penalties for even petty criminal behaviour had their origins in an idealist belief that doing away with exploitation and oppression would do away with crime and criminals. Any continuing manifestations were seen as legacies of the

87

past system, to be dealt with severely'. By the late 1970s, with the hindsight of the problems of socialist transition, legal codes and attitudes were more sophisticated, but new concepts such as 'social property' had led to particularly heavy penalties for crimes against this, as opposed to private property. 'We applied very severe sanctions for crimes which were really not so grave,' he said;

> It might have been something very small in terms of economic value. Consequently, there was a growing contradiction between the sanctions, the treatment of crime, and the social awareness. This created concern in government and among persons interested in justice... Experience has shown us that harsh sanctions did not serve as the slightest deterrent to crime...and the prison re-education system demonstrated to us that we were not dealing with criminals or persons who were morally corrupt. Rather, we were facing normal, common people, workers and youth, people who responded positively to re-education, who had simply made a mistake in their life and were not criminals as such. We had rare cases of recidivism when many of these people were released on parole, but we were giving them long sentences which were too severe. We were filling up the prisons with this kind of people.

The statistics showed that most thefts were of objects valued at less than 100 pesos. There was also a socio-economic reality: 'our stores are not full of electronic products, colour televisions, etc., things that consumer societies want and have. The majority of things stolen were of this kind — crimes motivated by youthful curiosity, desire.'

A study of 4,000 such cases led to reductions in sentences for over 1,000 people. Theft of social property could lead to sentences of 10-20 years. Now ten-year sentences have been reduced to three. The aggravating factor of theft of social property is ignored, though other factors such as force or assault still mean a much more severe sentence. Certain codes of conduct that have been declassified as crime, that is decriminalised, are to be dealt with by fines, probation and re-education in society. Just as within the mainstream jail system, high hopes are pinned on educative work, under the auspices of a new national commission for social prevention; and, while consumption needs cannot be met overnight, initiatives such as television and video rooms in the community and workplace can go a long way to help.

In a society striving for new values, adjustment is difficult, it is argued. Property can be nationalised by law, but attitudes cannot be changed simply through legislation. It takes a long process of education which is greatly determined by the economic base and development of society. Proportionately few of Cuba's criminals are women, but female prostitution is again a problem, the Deputy Minister admits. There were thousands of prostitutes before the revolution, and after 1959 it seemed to disappear as an institution. Yet a new phenomenon emerged:

> We now see a few young women who hang around the hotels, looking for tourists, to prostitute themselves, not for money but for material goods. It is a small number, but a new social phenomenon. When certain social or economic factors change, certain crimes, such as the previous form of prostitution, disappear because women no longer need to engage in it to survive economically. But with the development of new economic and social factors, it can re-emerge in a different form. The same holds for various kinds of crimes — theft of a tape recorder, a bicycle... We are convinced that with economic development, this situation will change, though of course, dialectically, we must be aware that other forms of behaviour may emerge... The percentage of traffic injuries increases each year. We are campaigning to raise awareness as to the responsibility of being behind a steering wheel. There used to be few accidents on horseback!... Education can go a long way, and we also need lawyers, courts and judges immersed in society's problems, closer to the people, not living in ivory towers.

4. Third World Power

'For Latin America, you represent the impassioned defence of our people's freedom and right to self-determination', said Mexican President Miguel de la Madrid in late 1988 when conferring the Aztec Eagle Order on Fidel Castro. 'The friendship between Mexico and Cuba goes back in time to the founders of our nationhood, those who fought for our independence over a century ago,' responded Castro in his speech of thanks, referring also to the Mexican revolution and the traditional relations between the two countries that had been maintained and even consolidated during the 30 years of Cuba's revolution. 'We are aware of the need to work together in these difficult times, to guarantee a future for each of our countries and our great common patrimony', he declared, receiving the award 'on behalf of all Cubans who have persevered in struggle, those who died and those who have carried on'.

To some extent, the sentiments can be judged in the context of statesmen's rhetoric. Yet they also echo deeply rooted national and international feelings that are being strengthened not only across the Gulf of Mexico to continental Latin America, but also across oceans, to Asia and Africa. Through its bilateral links with Third World governments and movements, and its principled stand in regional and international organisations on issues crucial to Third World interests, not least in its role as Chair of the Movement of Non-Aligned Countries, the relatively small island of Cuba has over the years established itself firmly as a leading Third World power.

To the West, Cuba has offered the spectre of military might, sending troops and ballistic support to violent conflict in Bolivia, Nicaragua, Angola, and Ethiopia, with numbers of troops that, if added up, would far outnumber the entire Cuban population. For the Third World, on the other hand, such active intervention has been only one contributing factor in Cuba's growing prestige. More essential has been its readiness to assist in economic and social terms, with material help as far as possible, but especially with human resources. Thousands of Cuba's doctors, nurses and teachers have exported practical assistance and have at the same time brought back to Cuba a growing body of first-hand knowledge of Third World problems absent in their own country today. The doctor who for the first time treats a starving child in northern Africa or the teacher who for the first time gives a class with no pencils or books on a dirt floor in Central America both come back changed by the experience, in the same way as the soldier who has fought alongside another people. That experience can be as traumatic as it is illuminating, but is one that has undoubtedly served overall to strengthen conviction in the face of injustice.

Nearly everyone in Cuba has some family member or friend who has been on international service — 300,000 civilian and military personnel over 13 years in Angola alone — and many more have volunteered. In a matter of days in 1979, 30,000 teachers had signed up to go to Nicaragua, and, when some of those that went were killed by the *contras*, a further 100,000 volunteered to take their place. The returnees recount exploits and hardships, share anecdotes and jokes, some funny, some crude. Stories might be partial, exaggerated and even prejudiced, but they help to penetrate that shroud of ignorance whereby Third World countries know more about imperial centres of power than they do about each other. Similarly, those from the Third World who go to study in Cuba — and they range from secondary to university students, trade union to peasant activists — take away with them more than subjects learned in the classroom. Not everything is easy; there are often mutual (especially cultural) incomprehensions, but the chance is afforded to experience Cuba's achievements and problems, and to analyse what is relevant or not to their own countries. Cuba's investments in the military, health and education have become more than a national resource. Even in strict economic terms, they are eminently exportable, but more important still is the interplay between the economic and the socio-political in both the domestic and international contexts, at the macro and micro level.

Developing Health Care

As the Cuban economy and people's living conditions have changed, so too the country's health profile and health care system have evolved in response to new pressures and new needs. Health care is considered to be a state responsibility and the right of the people;

Julio Etchart

Mayday, Havana, 1988

access is guaranteed free of charge, with integrated preventive and curative services. These basic principles have not changed, but organisational structures and strategies have, as determined by the priorities of the moment. A dynamism and somewhat unorthodox popular participation has led to phases of development very different from more traditional medical practice. By the mid-1980s, dramatic changes were taking place at both ends of the medical care spectrum; at the level of primary care Cuba adopted the use of family practitioners, while, simultaneously, great attention and resources were being devoted to sophisticated, expensive and technologically intense tertiary care and research.

In the initial decade of the 1960s, the obvious tasks were to deliver as much curative care as possible to a population suffering from acutely infectious diseases, to develop a coherent national network of services, and to train large numbers of health personnel to cover for the exodus of some 3,000 of the country's 6,000 physicians. In order to solve problems of high mortality and morbidity, resources were devoted to maternal-child health and disease-specific campaigns coordinated at the national and local levels. They targeted particular problems and under-served areas, and attempted to integrate various existing health facilities into a state system. The single system was consolidated by the late 1960s, and the 1970s were devoted to better organised medicine in the community, through specialist services at the polyclinic level. Mortality and morbidity rates fell steadily, life expectancy increased, and the emphasis began to change from curative to preventive care. The one major criticism by the 1980s was that the clinic was not small enough to facilitate the integration of health personnel with the community they served, resulting in specialist fragmentation and continued overuse of hospitals where top specialists could be found, little continuity of care, and deficiencies in preventive medicine such as immunisation and screening. In the absence of nationwide surveys, risk factors such as hypertension or obesity went under-reported. New morbidity profiles involved chronic diseases that kill at a later age and require early, carefully planned, long-term preventive strategies, illnesses less amenable to quick, low-technology cures and involving damaging occupational, environmental and behavioural patterns that the clinic was ill-equipped to assess.

The start of the Family Doctor programme in 1985 marked as profound a change again. By gradually introducing the structure of a doctor living and working directly with 120 families, or 600-700 people, the number of practising physicians will be roughly doubled. Similarly, there will be increased nursing staff, a changing role for the polyclinic and readjusted procedures throughout the system. Based on an exact census of their populations, family doctors do continuous community diagnosis of their area, collecting health and socio-economic information for every person, sick and healthy. For the first time, the well population has become part of the health workers' brief, providing a data base which resembles an epidemiologist's dream. For the system to work, however, there must also be the curative resources and facilities at the point of referral: effective heart disease and cancer therapies, tissue and organ transplants, and microsurgery.

Interestingly, just as current complaints of strains at the intermediate polyclinic level will no doubt result in changes there, the changes that have been made at both ends of the system came in response to unrest and dissatisfaction expressed by the population for better specialist and better community service. Likewise, both the range of health experience and the new developments in primary and tertiary care can help meet Cuba's explicitly stated goal of becoming a 'medical power', capable of providing the expertise and technology transfer that other developing countries may need. The extent to which it can do so effectively depends also on the collective experience of the thousands of medical personnel it has abroad, contributing to information and scientific progress in all areas. One example would be that of the Cuban team at the children's orthopaedic hospital at Baghdad, Iraq, who since 1978 have been faced with polio, cerebral palsy and feet deformities, as well as needs in traumatology, physiotherapy and prosthesis. The team provides the health care while also training Iraqi professionals.

At present, Cuba has over 31,000 physicians, including 6,000 family doctors (increasing at the rate of 2,000 a year) and 3,000 working in some 30 foreign countries. The total figure includes the 3,440 graduates for l988 of the first contingent of the Carlos J. Finlay Medical Detachment, 2,000 of whom are now working in Cuba as family doctors, and a further 80 on internationalist service in Zambia. A total of 147 graduates of the contingent came from 45 different countries, mainly African and Latin American. Set up six years ago to prepare community doctors at both home and abroad, the detachment was named after Cuba's eminent 19th-century physician who discovered the mosquito vector of yellow fever. Members of its first Ernesto Che Guevara contingent see themselves as the 'new kind of dedicated doctor', as Yamila de Armas, of Cienfuegos, put it, looking forward to being a family doctor in the small town of Cruces. Raúl González Torres, who did his intern year at a rural hospital in the mountains behind Guantánamo, spoke of how 'the different health problems of the rural population' he faced, helped prepare him better as an all-round doctor. Rafael Lugo Fernández, about to go to Zambia, similarly described how important being an internationalist was to his medical training.

Aside from service of this nature, Cuba has developed a capacity to mobilise quickly in emergency and national disaster, as in the case of two events in 1988. Having been successfully eradicated from Cuba, dengue disease suddenly struck again in epidemic proportions in the early l980s. Common to many other underdeveloped countries, dengue is transmitted by a particular type of mosquito; it causes fever, headache, pain, gastro-intestinal disorders and other symptoms, and can be fatal. Its eradication required extensive curative emergency care and longer-term health and hygiene measures to keep the mosquito from breeding. Special mosquito para-health brigades were formed to carry out periodic fumigation checks in risk areas. A 1988 outbreak of dengue in Ecuador, especially in the slum areas of Guayaquil, prompted Cuba to send doctors, scientists and a 100-strong health brigade, plus equipment, insecticides and larvicides. 250,000 homes were fumigated, and pools and puddles, the breeding ground for larvae, were eliminated. The Ecuadorean health minister described the speed and efficiency with which the Cuban government acted as 'decisive' in wiping out the disease.

When, in October l988, Hurricane Joan hit Nicaragua, Cuba immediately sent aid in the form of evacuation personnel. They were followed by a brigade of Cuban surgeons, epidemiologists, pediatricians, technicians, and support personnel from the Cuban Red Cross that was formed within 12 hours and flown into the Bluefields disaster zone with medicines, plasma, vaccines, first-aid materials and food. This was the first relief to reach Nicaragua from abroad, and the first of an initial seven Cuban flights with food, medicine and specialised personnel.

The flow is two-way: Cuban health personnel to other countries, and patients to Cuba. A development in the 1980s has been a 'health tourism' plan, whereby Cuban health facilities can be used for a reasonable price that includes a hotel package for patients not requiring hospitalisation and their companions. In more needy cases, health care is provided free of charge. On an individual level, such cases in l986-7 ranged from a seven-year-old British girl suffering from vitiligo to four Ecuadorean slum children badly burned after an explosion in a warehouse where they were playing.

Of the many more collective initiatives, there is a camp near Havana that houses some 200 Salvadorean war-wounded. Most of

Hugh O'Shaughnessy/The Observer

Young FMLN veteran, Santiago de las Vegas

them are under 20, and many are mutilated, with missing limbs or lost eye-sight. A first group arrived in Cuba in 1985, under an exchange of prisoners between the Salvadorean regime and the Farabundo Martí National Liberation Front (FMLN) involving the release of the kidnapped daughter of President Napoleón Duarte. A second group arrived in 1987, by virtue of the Geneva agreements on war wounded. 'The medical treatment they receive here', according to Nelia Lopéz, the Cuban nurse in charge of the camp's patients, 'involves much more than sewing up wounds, applying physiotherapy, easing pain or restoring tissue. They must learn to live with their disabilities, and we must help keep up their spirits'. The Salvadoreans came to a large old house, two wooden dormitories and a clinic. They themselves have since built three more dormitories, classrooms, a dining room and recreation facilities, and they are working on playing fields, an exhibition area, and a lecture room. Longer-term construction plans include a whole hospital for Salvadoreans in Havana.

Studying on the Island

It is popularly referred to as 'la isla' — not the main island of Cuba, but a smaller one to the south of Havana province, today called the Isle of Youth. Its past infamy was due to the location there of the Model Prison, where convicts (including Castro in the 1950s) were sent for hard labour. In the 1960s, it was singled out as a citrus and dairy development area, and some of Havana's delinquents went there to work. A continued spur to development came in the 1970s, with the arrival of thousands of Havana secondary level students in new boarding schools in the countryside. They were in the classroom for half the day, and in the citrus groves and on the dairy farms for the other half. The prison fell into disuse and was then turned into a museum and Pioneer Palace for students; the island became a national, then an international, school community.

The idea of the international schools first arose in June 1977, when Cuba offered the newly liberated Angola of President Agostinho Neto four schools on the Isle of Youth, with space for 600 Angolan students in each. In the event, the first students were Angolan, Namibian and Mozambican. In October 1987, addressing a rally on the Isle to commemorate the tenth anniversary of the first internationalist intake, Jorge Risquet, Party Political Bureau member for African affairs, recalled the origins of the schools:

...our friends from Mozambique heard about the offer and Comrade Samora Machel asked Fidel if Mozambique could also send children to the Isle... It was around then, on May 5, 1977, to be precise, that there was the vicious South African attack on Namibian refugee camps in southern Angola, the horrific Kassinga massacre killing over 500 women, children and elderly... A few dozen children managed to escape. However, there were many other camps in southern Angola, and it was felt that children there were in imminent danger if the forces of racist South Africa were to carry out another attack of the same kind... That is why we started to gather together all the Namibian children who were in southern Angola, and send them to Luanda, from there to Havana, and from Havana to the Isle of Youth.

The difficulties were not to be underestimated. It was decided, given the multiplicity of dialects the children spoke (such that children from the same country often could not communicate), that they would learn the prevailing language in their respective countries. This was English in the case of Namibia, and Portuguese for Angola and Mozambique. They would also be taught history and geography by teachers of their respective nationalities, and were to be encouraged to develop (and share) their cultures and ways. The majority of general subjects would be taught in Spanish by Cuban teachers.

The experience of the internal running of the schools and their insertion into the wider community has inevitably involved a certain amount of trial and error. A whole infrastructure of health and services needed to be tailored to their needs. There also had to be a process of mutual learning and respect, not only from students, teachers and other staff, but also from the relatively small island population of 58,000 that has had to assimilate the growing student influx. The capital, Nueva Gerona, once a sleepy backwater linked by slow ferry to the Cuban southern coast fishing town of Batabanó, has grown rapidly to become one of the country's most cosmopolitan Third World centres, with new hotels and additional hydrofoil services from Batabanó, plus daily flights direct from Havana. Not without reason, in the politico-administrative division of the country, the Isle of Youth qualifies as a special municipality, on a par with the other 14 provinces.

The 1987-8 international enrolment figures stood at 16,000 students from 37 countries: 1,922 in elementary school, 9,151 in junior high, 1,975 in senior high, 2,305 in polytechnics and some 700 at the university-level Institute of Pedagogy. That year there were schools exclusively for students from Namibia, Angola, Ghana, Ethiopia, the Congo, Guinea-Bissau, the Saharawi Arab Democratic Republic, Mozambique, the Democratic People's Republic of Korea and

Nicaragua (with a South Africa/ANC Nelson Mandela school scheduled to open in 1988-9); a special multi-nation Vanguard of Havana senior high school, with students from the Sahara, the Congo, Guinea-Bissau, São Tomé, Ethiopia, Angola, Mozambique, Cape Verde, Nicaragua and Guatemala; two polytechnics specialising in economics with students also from Equatorial Guinea, Sierra Leone, Lesotho, Burundi, Panama and Democratic Yemen; and special day-care provision for the children of teachers and mature students. All the schools are built and organised along much the same lines as the rest of Cuba's schools in the countryside, with the exception that students cannot go home at weekends. They live in, sleeping in dormitories on the school premises, spending half their days in the classroom and the other half in the fields, thereby making some contribution to the economy and also to their own upkeep by growing vegetables for their own consumption. The Cuban state provides virtually everything else: the buildings, uniforms, materials, and a stipend.

There are complaints from the students about the food, lack of privacy, and shortness of money and outside entertainment (although excursions and inter-school friendship events are organised). Some students have more access than others to hard currency and the goods it can buy, and there are those who are tempted into small-scale marketing on the side, creating problems within the student body and also among the wider Cuban population that does not have similar access. But the moral pressures on them are great, since they are being clothed, housed and fed, and receiving an education with a security they could hardly expect in their own countries. More to the concern of the educators and governments involved are the potential longer-term psycho-social dislocations involved in divorcing students from their home environment over a crucial formative period, and their eventual insertion back into it after a long absence. Another less openly acknowledged problem is the occasional hostility and racism encountered by some students from sections of the Cuban population who are clearly resentful of what they see as the students' relatively privileged position.

Among the most sought-after careers for students who go on to university are medicine, agriculture, veterinary medicine, economics, engineering and education. This last is also partly catered for on the island, since a physics and mathematics annex of the University of Havana Institute of Pedagogy opened in the 1986-7 academic year, to be followed by another for biology, chemistry and geography. Osmin Viera, the dean of the Institute, speaks highly of his African intake: 'They are systematic in study for they see teaching as fundamental to the development of their countries'. He is experienced in this field, for he was once a student himself at the Vanguard of Havana multi-nation school.

Founded in 1972, initially for students from Havana, the school took its first group of Nicaraguans after the 1979 Nicaraguan revolution. 'That is when the seed of integration was planted', says the current vice-principal Gabriel Carillo. With its eleven nationalities today, the school has a teaching staff of 38 Cubans, as well as teachers from the Sahara, Guinea-Bissau and Nicaragua. Spanish is the basic language, but some nationalities have classes in English and Arabic. The school's Student Council has representatives from each of the nationalities, and its president attends all meetings of the school board of directors. 'A miniature United Nations of developing countries', it was once aptly called by visiting Robert Mugabe.

From Kassinga to Cuito Cuanavale

Henrick Witbooi is the name of one of the veteran schools for Namibians (184 boys and 189 girls), which has seen students who first came to elementary school graduate to university. One of its teachers, Martin Chibolo, travelled to Cuba in 1978 with child survivors of Kassinga. A member of the South West Africa People's Organisation (SWAPO), he sees his work as preparing for rebuilding an independent Namibia:

> The situation is abnormal in Namibia. We do not have universities and the high schools are closed. We never dreamed that during our struggle we could have schools like these for the Namibian children. The South African racists, of all people, claim the children are sent here to work like slaves in the fields. Can a slave become a doctor, a teacher, an engineer? For very soon now we will have doctors, teachers and engineers who graduated in Cuba. The racists will find that SWAPO has educated its children and will be ready to rebuild Namibia once independence is achieved.

Events involving Cuba in the southern cone of Africa in 1987-8 brought that independence closer than ever before. In late 1987, Angolan government forces fighting UNITA rebels near the south-eastern border with Namibia, far from the strategic Cuban lines, were driven back by a massive South African military intervention, involving 9,000 troops, tanks and other armoured vehicles, long-range artillery and fighter planes. Angola's best units were besieged in the town of Cuito Cuanavale by forces 6,000-strong and were in danger of being wiped out. Such defeat would have been

101

disastrous for Angola, for it meant the possible destruction of independence. At the time, no Cuban advisers, troops or other military personnel were in Cuito Cuanavale but, at the request of the Angolan government, advisers were sent there in December, and, in January 1988, motorised infantry units, tanks and artillery arrived to provide military support. Cuban help was requested, as it had originally been after Angolan independence in 1975, to assist the African state out of a difficult situation, but this time it was also needed to ensure the security of the Cuban troops themselves.

A massive logistical reinforcement operation, involving armoured units and anti-aircraft weapons, went into action. In a record number of weeks, troops and construction workers built air bases in Cahama and Menongue. A combined Angolan-Cuban air and land operation defended Cuito Cuanavale from repeated South African attack, making a mockery of South African claims that it had been captured in January 1988. By March, the siege was lifted, and Cuban-Angolan-SWAPO forces on the western flank of southern Angola subsequently drove South African forces 250 kilometers back to the border with occupied Namibia.

The result was a military victory of such proportions as to change the entire state of play in southern Africa. It left Angola in a position of strength, with better equipped conventional forces; it provided a decorous basis for the withdrawal of Cuban troops; and it caused the South African-Angolan negotiations to develop in the summer of 1988 into the four-sided Angolan/Cuban-South African/US talks in London, Cairo, Washington and Brazzaville, subsequently involving the USSR in the Brazzaville follow-up meeting in November. No longer was Angola to be beaten back on demands for unilateral concessions while suffering continued South African incursions. The balance of forces had tipped in favour of a solution based on UN Security Council Resolution 435 (on the statute books since 1978), with independence for Namibia, security for Angola and peace in south-west Africa.

It is very much recognised from the Angolan and Cuban sides that there have to be third-party guarantees for South African non-aggression, for, as long as apartheid continues, there is a threat to all Front Line States. Similarly, Angola defends its prerogative to request Cuban reinforcements whenever there is renewed South African military escalation. Another point on the agenda has been the release and/or exchange of prisoners of war, such as South African Sergeant Johan Papenfus who was receiving medical care in Havana's Hermanos Amejeiras hospital, Cuban prisoner Orlando Cardoso held in Somalia from 1978-88, and pilots Lieutenant Colonel

Manuel Rojas García and Captain Ramón Quesada shot down and held prisoner by UNITA from October 1987 to August 1988. The Cuban withdrawal will have UN monitoring, most probably with Soviet and US representatives involved.

The war has produced mixed feelings and reactions in Cuba. There is understandable patriotic pride that Cuban military prowess has played a key role in deterring the best-equipped army in Africa. There is also considerable anxiety concerning the welfare of Cuban combatants on the part of their friends and families. Such anxiety is in part fuelled by what has been an almost complete black-out on news from war zones in Angola. Major coverage tends to come late, in the build-up to or the successful completion of a military action, and until recently rarely gave details of Cuban losses. The authorities can defend this self-censorship in the same way as any other state does when engaged in war. First-hand accounts are, of course, what bring the war home. One such account was that published by *Bastión*, the newspaper of the armed forces, on First Lieutenant Benito Tena Macías, holder of the International Fighter, First Class, and Defence of Cuito Cuanavale medals. Tena Macías was one of the Cuban advisers posted to the Angolan army's 59th Infantry Brigade defence line. Wounded by enemy mortar fire, he fought on for the rest of the day before crawling several kilometers to the Cuban-Angolan lines.

Such tales of patriotic valour are reminiscent of stories that emerged out of Grenada at the time of the US invasion in 1983, when a number of Cuban construction workers were killed in conflict with US paratroopers. In the case of Grenada, however, the odds were overwhelming and the situation unclear after Maurice Bishop's murder, allegedly by an opposing faction of the ruling New Jewel Movement. The military battle was therefore impossible, but the sense of loss among Cubans for a fellow Caribbean people was as great as was their earlier wrath over Mariel. In the case of Angola, however, what should not be underestimated is Cuba's sense not only of the present-day connections, but also historical roots. The Cubans see themselves very much as a Latin-African people, with a rich common heritage, extending from music and dance to food and linguistic expressions. While some complain about fighting another's war, many others see their role as atoning for slavery, colonialism and neocolonialism by helping to prepare Angola for greater self-sufficiency in the future. Whatever the early Cuban observations of a lack of Angolan military spirit (skilled as the Angolan fighters were in guerrilla but not conventional warfare), the end result of

103

over a decade of Cuban military aid has been to train a conventional defence force which is certainly one step in that direction.

The real culprit in the dirty war against Angola, like that against Nicaragua, is seen in Havana as the US, playing part mediator, part belligerent. While supporting peace initiatives — whether the multilateral agreement on Angola, the Arias peace plan for Central America, Esquipulas or Sapoá for Nicaragua — the US has also promoted so-called low-intensity conflict and dirty wars against small progressive governments, whether in Central America or Africa. The double standards, according to the Cuban government, extend to the way in which the Reagan administration embraced *detente* with the USSR, but has remained implacably hostile towards Cuba. The suspicion that Washington treats Third World socialist states differently from those of the Eastern bloc has confirmed Cuban readiness to resort to military tactics, if necessary. The military option is hardly economically viable for Cuba, but is one, Castro stated again in December 1988, that the country is compelled to take for its own defence, reserving the right to assist in the defence of other small developing countries, if at their request. In the case of Angola, the strain on Cuba's resources has been inestimable, not least on the people themselves, those who go and the families they leave behind. Few would argue, however, that the precondition for demilitarisation is anything other than US acceptance of the existence of progressive, independent nations, socialist or otherwise, with sovereign relations between them.

Of potentially far greater scope than the military victory in Angola, will be the social and economic consequences of a peace agreement. Judging from the experience in Ethiopia and Nicaragua, economic relations between Cuba and Angola will increase as Cuba's military presence declines. Its economic, scientific and technical cooperation with the developing world has its roots precisely on the African continent in the 1960s, largely with Algeria and Guinea. In the 1970s cooperation increased rapidly to include 27 African and Middle Eastern countries, 37 by 1988. The main areas of Cuban assistance, aside from health and education, have been agriculture, construction, transport and communications, fishing, heavy and light industry. Payment has been operated on a sliding scale, or in kind, while in more needy cases, donations are given — sugar, medicines and tinned milk to Indochina in the 1960s — which expanded to full-scale donations of hospitals and agricultural and communications projects to independent Vietnam after 1973, along with similar aid to Laos.

When Cuba entered the socialist bloc's COMECON in 1972, a new phase began in international assistance, with the island more on the receiving than the giving end, on a similar scale of values: i.e. cooperation designed to bring the less developed countries closer to the levels of the more developed, in which sugar, citrus and nickel played an important initial role. This in turn enabled Cuba to play a more active role of assistance to other parts of the developing world. In the case of Angola, the 1988 trade agreements already covered sugar, fish, medicines, books and toys, and agricultural implements, while, under technical assistance programmes in action since 1976, more than 2,000 Cubans were already working in Angola. They included doctors, nurses, teachers, sugar specialists, pulp and paper personnel, lumberjacks, and construction workers who have over the years spent much of their energies on rebuilding bridges destroyed by enemy action.

The Non-Aligned, Debt and Disarmament

Growing collaboration of this kind is South-South dialogue in action, but Cuba, Angola and many other Third World countries are clear that this on its own own is not enough. Central to their analysis of a better future are peace, reduced military spending, and nuclear disarmament, as are also an end to foreign debt and the beginnings of a new international economic order. These issues have emerged in all major Third World bloc meetings, most importantly of all perhaps being that of the Movement of Non-Aligned Countries. Little is heard about the movement in the West, and yet, in approximately the same time span as the Cuban revolution and with Cuba as a founding member and playing a prominent role (it was elected Chair from 1979-83), the movement grew from a membership of 25 countries in its founding year of 1961 to 101 in 1988, contributing to a vastly changing international community as seen at the UN. The non-aligned movement's growth is linked to the post-1960 Third World phenomenon of political decolonisation (i.e formal independence, accompanied or not by popular and military struggle) and economic recolonisation (through trade, debt and intensified politico-military conflict). This has centred particularly on African and Asian countries, though the movement itself extends to Europe and Latin America as well, thereby embracing the long-independent to the newly nationalist, through many shades of the political spectrum.

The seeds of the movement were sown at the Afro-Asian Conference in Bandung, Indonesia, in 1955, out of which came the concepts of Third World, economic underdevelopment and non-alignment from major powers. Its concern was for those fundamental rights embodied in the UN Charter of peoples and nations to self-determination, economic development and cooperation, focusing special concern on the problems of dependent peoples and the need for world peace. Leadership came from Egypt's Nasser, India's Nehru and Yugoslavia's Tito. By 1960, at the 15th UN General Assembly, it was clear that the numerical balance was shifting with the 17 new member countries of Asia and Africa, plus the presence of revolutionary Cuba.

In 1961, the non-aligned movement was formed in Belgrade by 25 countries, including three Latin American observers (Bolivia, Brazil and Ecuador), and representatives of 35 national liberation movements, political parties and related organisations. The meeting declared its support for independence and for colonial peoples, its opposition to military action against non-independent countries and peoples, condemnation of the events in Angola and South Africa, and its recognition of the rights of people to self-determination — as in the case of Cuba. The First and Second Declarations of Havana, in 1960 and 1962, were well within the non-aligned brief.

Cairo hosted a conference in 1962 on the problems of economic development and out of the Cairo 1964 2nd Summit came an economic action programme. Membership had already grown to 47 (29 from Africa, 15 from Asia, ten from Latin America and three from Europe) with ten observers. By the Lusaka 3rd Summit of 1970 there were 54 full members, and key issues were the Near East, Indochina, apartheid, the decolonisation of Portuguese-held Angola, Morocco and Guinea, Zimbabwe and Namibia, disarmament, the situation in Cyprus, and the widening gap between the developed and the underdeveloped worlds. An international development strategy focused on raw materials, the net flow of financial transfers, debt-servicing and the adjustment of developed countries' productive structure for technology transfers, all of which had its influence on UN bodies such as UNCTAD, UNDP, and ECLA.

At the Algiers 1973 summit, it was Castro who noted the coincidence of positions on many issues between non-aligned and socialist countries, describing them as 'natural allies'. The economic action programme that year was designed to promote cooperation, and lobby for a new international monetary system. This was carried over to the UN General Assembly in the form of demands for a new international economic order, with the support of the underdeveloped world and the socialist bloc. And, at the 1975 Havana Non-Aligned Coordinating Bureau and Lima Committee of Experts meetings, the movement laid down ground rules for treating foreign capital and for solidarity among members under pressure for

Laurie Sparham/Network

1979 Non-Aligned Summit, Havana

their exercise of sovereignty. Little wonder, then, that while Cuba was being seriously questioned over its 'non-alignment' from the Soviet Union. the Cuban decision over Angola was seen as a sovereign decision and well received by many member countries.

By the 1976 Sri Lanka summit, at which 86 countries were represented, it was clear that the socialist camp was warming to the movement, while the capitalist countries were standing off. Areas of special concern were South Africa, Palestine, the Middle East, Cyprus, Korea and Latin America, disarmament and international security, and the phenomenal rise of the underdeveloped countries' balance of payments problem.

The 1979 Havana summit, which ushered in Cuba as Chair and had a stronger Latin American presence, paid special emphasis to Latin American problems. Economic issues were overshadowed by world, regional and local political issues, with an absence of agreement between members (not least Yugoslavia and Cuba) but what has been called 'civilised disagreement', maintaining the movement's unity. Even so, there was support for Nicaragua, Grenada and the people's struggle in El Salvador, and condemnation for such regimes as in Guatemala.

The 1983 New Delhi summit saw a dramatic shift in emphasis to the economic, and was where Castro gave his landmark speech on the global economic crisis, the debt and the new international economic order, at the end of Cuba's mandate. Since then, leading up to and since the 1987 summit in Harare, Zimbabwe, this politico-economic issue has been a major one for the movement, and has been increasingly linked to demilitarisation and disarmament, to prevent nuclear war. A special non-aligned ministerial meeting on disarmament was held in Havana in May 1988, out of which came the Havana Appeal to the Moscow Summit for bilateral negotiations to lead to more multilateral negotiations, especially within the UN, and for peace to be accompanied by non-intervention and non-interference based on the elimination of colonialism, foreign domination and occupation, apartheid, with the freeing of military expenditures of the great powers for economic and social development, but the right of small powers to maintain their legitimate defence. This was subsequently ratified at the September Cyprus Coordinating Bureau meeting. The post-disarmament issue of debt and the new international economic order is one that is catapulting Latin America to new prominence within the movement and has brought Cuba back firmly within the Latin American fold.

Latin American Overtures

The 1960s saw Cuba isolated within the Western Hemisphere, driven out of the Organisation of American States, its trade and diplomatic relations severed by virtually all the Americas. Its links were with the more progressive elements, and in some cases guerrilla *focos* (in line with the Guevarist will to 'create one, two, three...Vietnams', to weaken imperialism by making it fight on many fronts), which were themselves under considerable hostile pressure. With the strengthening of right-wing Latin American dictatorships in the 1970s, Cuba was seen to 'pull out' of its involvement in Latin America and 'go into' Africa, with increasing aid to other nascent African states. The 1980s have witnessed a growing coincidence of views between Cuba and Latin America, at regional and national governmental and non-governmental levels, bringing into play new progressive civilian regimes and activist groupings. Havana has served to host several major debt conferences, and the Latin American *rapprochement* over the major Latin American debt is being seen as a new rallying cry to both Pan-Americanism and Third Worldism.

The first call to Pan-Americanism came in 1826 from Latin America's early 19th-century independence fighter Simón Bolívar. His concept was one of a Latin American unity of the newly independent republics. By the end of the century, on the wave of considerable political and economic expansion within the hemisphere, the US had developed a Pan-Americanism invoking the Monroe Doctrine and manifest destiny in Latin America, and out of this came Inter-Americanism and the Organisation of American States. However, it was the political nature of US aid in the post-war era the Marshall plan for Europe that led to the UN's ECLA and new notions of Latin American unity: the Latin American Free Trade Association in 1960, the Andean countries' sub-group in 1969, the Group of 77 at the UN from 1970, reflecting Latin American dissatisfaction over the developed countries' aid and trade concessions; and in 1975 SELA (Latin American Economic System) with its various affiliate bodies for Latin American and South-South integration. A sign of Latin America's increasing insertion into Third World issues was the 1978 founding of the Latin American Association of Afro-Asian Studies in Mexico. In the context of these developments, the debt (and Cuba) was to be the major 1980s integrationist boost, with mooted opposition to and even exclusion of the US from regional organisations.

The integrationist impetus has been fuelled by powerful political conflicts, especially the issue of Central America, the Falklands/Malvinas war of 1982 and Panama's sovereignty over the canal zone, which has met with strong opposition from the US and seen the murder of nationalist military leader Omar Torrijos and the discrediting of his successor Manuel Antonio Noriega on drug charges. The US campaign, Cuba alleges, is tied up with the military bases in the canal zone which under the 1979 Torrijos-Carter treaties are referred to as 'revertible areas'. The Central America situation and new agreements on intermediate and short-range missiles have brought conventional warfare back into greater prominence within US defence strategy, and lend new importance to bases like those in Panama.

Cuba's strong position on each of these issues, along with the wider one of debt, was the backdrop to two major visits by Castro to Latin

---

The Politics of Sport

For controversial political reasons, Cuba did not attend the Olympic Games in either 1984 or 1988. The 1984 Games were held in the US, and Cuba's position was in solidarity with a decision by the Eastern European socialist bloc not to attend on grounds of security. The 1988 Games were held in South Korea, after a long battle within the Olympic movement over their being co-hosted by North Korea. Cuba was an ardent champion of that movement, in keeping with its and the non-aligned position on the repressive nature of the US-backed Seoul regime and the Korean national question. However, it found itself almost alone within the socialist camp, as only Cuba, Albania and North Korea went through with a boycott.

Speaking at an honorary medal-giving ceremony in Havana at the time of the 1988 Olympics, amidst tight, minimal news coverage of the Games, Castro was at pains to point out that security was not the issue. It was a matter of international principles, he declared. His displeasure over the eastern socialist bloc's attendance was scarcely veiled and led him to stress Cuba's 'non-alignment'. He also added fire to Cuba's growing voice against the increasing commercialisation of Olympic sports. The fine notion behind the Olympics, he argued, had been turned into the prerogative of rich nations. Colossal sums made out of the Olympics could go toward building up sport and installations, and the ultimate hosting of games in the Third World. How many medals do Third World countries win? Very few: they have few sports installations, few instructors, an inadequate standard of living to form the backdrop to a sound sports movement. Without food, how can

---

America: in August to Ecuador for the inauguration of President Rodrigo Borja (an occasion for Ecuador to re-establish diplomatic relations with Nicaragua) and in November to Mexico for the presidential inauguration of Carlos Salinas de Gortari. With the exception of a two-day visit to Mexico in 1981, they were his first visits since Chile under Allende in 1972 and Nicaragua under Ortega in 1983. Each elicted evident signs of sympathies from broad sectors of opinion towards the Cuban position as holding the key to a Pan Americanism in keeping with the 1980s.

As regards the debt, the Cuban starting-point is to set the issue and the concept of a crisis in their correct context. The 1986 US$1 trillion (US$1 million millions) Third World debt is not, it is argued, a very significant sum in world terms. The US debt is twice that; or, put another way, the Third World debt is only one-third of the annual turnover of the world's top 200 transnationals, one eighth of the

---

they have champions?, he asked. The Olympics have become an instrument fuelling theories of national and racial superiority. If Third World countries had the conditions, logic has it that the rich nations of today would get very few medals.

Not going to Los Angeles and then Seoul, was for Cuba a considerable sacrifice and controversial among the island's many sports lovers. The build-up of Cuban sports over the last three decades has resulted in a mass amateur movement (professional sport is banned) that spans old favourites like baseball to the newly popular soccer (Brazil's Pele and Argentina's Maradona have contributed to its growing popularity) volleyball, basketball, athletics, boxing, fencing, diving and chess, with games and exercise taken seriously from kindergarten to schools for the disabled, mental institutions, and clubs for the elderly. It has also reaped national, regional and world records (boxer Stevenson and sprinter Juantorena will be names that spring to mind), putting Cuba well on the map among Third World countries for medals and sports cooperation (a Cuban basketball coach for Brazil in exchange for a Brazilian soccer coach in Cuba).

Having successfully hosted the 1982 Central American Games, Cuba is currently defending its right to host the 1991 Pan American Games, in the light of its non-attendance at what Cuban Olympic Committee President Manuel González Guerra called the anti-Olympics of Seoul. Work is pressing ahead on new installations for the games in Havana, and so far, there has been overwhelming support from Latin American Olympic national committees, including those of such less likely parts as Chile and Guatemala.

annual Gross National Product (GNP) generated by the 24 rich nations of the Organisation for Economic Cooperation and Development. Third World loan financing, the argument goes, went into mimic modernisation and wasteful consumption, but above all into capital flight out of the debtor countries and militarisation: US$10,000 million of Argentina's US$59,000 million debt is directly related to the military, while Brazil was helped into the debt trap by arms budgets that it is now paying back, thanks in part to arms exports. The bulk of lending has come from Western banks, with little foresight or consideration for the social implications of their actions. US lending in the Third World, for instance, leapt by 300 per cent between 1978 and 1982, with little concern for repayment viability. Mexico's defaulting in 1982, the nationalisation of the banks and enforced exchange controls, thus came as a major shock to the system, precipitating a 'crisis', Cuba insists, which was not of the majority of people's making.

What makes the Latin American debt particularly striking is that the continent is rich in comparison with the rest of the world: according to 1980s World Bank figures, the Latin American *per capita* GNP topped US$1,700 (well over US$2,000 for Argentina, Mexico and Venezuela), compared with US$220 for the sub-Sahara. However, within the region there is marked inequality between countries: Brazil's *per capita* GNP of over US$1,700 compares with Bolivia's US$509; Panama's US$2,200, with Honduras's US$721 and Haiti's US$320. There is an even more marked disparity between social classes within the countries; Mexico, Brazil and Venezuela are notorious for unequal income distribution, with flamboyant elite life-styles alongside rising infant mortality and malnutrition among the poor.

Viewed from the South, there has been one constant in the debt process: a net exodus of resources from the Third World to the First, thereby helping to prop up the centres of finance during a period in which the developed Western economies have undergone profound and often traumatic shifts in structure. The net capital outflow from Latin America alone between 1982 and 1985 was US$106,000 million, while in 1988 the World Bank calculated that the Third World as a whole had sent US$143,000 million to the developed West since 1983. As a result, in 1985, Latin American net *per capita* GNP was nine per cent lower than it had been in 1980. Mexico's decision to default and set up its own Central Bank holding funds in the country until currency reserves were up was just the start of a chain. Peru decided to limit debt payments to ten per cent of export revenues, with a new populist debt package geared to alleviating poverty and hunger. The

Cartagena Group, meanwhile, was envisaged as a cartel of the big 11 Latin American debtors.

Cuba, however, has simply advocated that the debt is unpayable and uncollectable, that there should be a cancellation, not a moratorium, that the debtors' slate should be wiped clean. Critics have claimed that Cuba can afford to proselytise, since it does not face the problems confronting its Latin American neighbours and that it has a more affordable debt. In response, Castro has stated that Cuba must honour its debt to the West, since creditor countries lent money to Cuba in defiance of US policies of embargo, and that every attempt is made to manage repayments without any negative repercussions on the welfare of the Cuban people, although the strain is clearly great. The Cuban position within a wider context is clear: that Third World governments and peoples have only one option, that of lobbying for non-payment of the debt as a pre-condition for an international reordering of economic objectives, peace and disarmament.

Within Cuba, as elsewhere, the calls for action range from the impassioned to the rational; they come from various social sectors including the religious community and the women's movement, farmers and workers. 'We do not accept the false reasoning of the force of arms over the legitimate force of reason that is the right to life', is the position of the Cuban Christian ecumenical community. More unequivocal in their indictment of the US and its policies are the words of Oden Marichal, vice-rector of the Matanzas Theological Seminary and Cuban coordinator of the Caribbean Conference of Churches: 'Christians of Central America and the Caribbean must mobilise to unmask imperialism, with its lies aimed at confusing US and world public opinion. We Christians must fight for peace, which is to fight for life, for there can be no safe refuge from war, save peace'. Religious women are also making their voice heard. Dora Valentín, women's coordinator for Latin America and the Caribbean, spoke at a continental meeting for peace of how 'the shattered peace of our area calls on Christian women to mobilise more and more against the forces of aggression to defend peace at all costs. We have an important contribution to make regarding the pressing economic, social and political change our society needs.'

The extent to which such dimensions of change are seen as interrelated was encapsulated in the words of Havana's Archbishop, Monsignor Jaime Ortega:

> How can the Church fulfill its mission at the service of a world divided into different social classes, and how can it do so when it itself is divided

113

by the class struggle? Cuban Catholics are aware that we are part of a world that seems to be closed in on itself and at times without any sense of the importance of life and events, caught up in a frightening arms race, while two-thirds of humanity go hungry and bear on their shoulders the well-being of the rest... As a member of the Latin American church, we feel as our own the hopes and anguish of Latin America. We experience the same concern over its tragic economic situation, worsened by a foreign debt of fantastic proportions whose payment under current conditions would bring dire poverty for our countries. In my view, payment is ethically unjustifiable, just like the present international economic order... Socialism has taught us to give out of justice what formerly we only gave out of charity.

Lázaro Domínguez, of the Secretariat of the CTC, expands on this reasoning: 'A major problem today, and one that is related to the foreign debt, is world *detente*, the solution to old conflicts such as Afghanistan, Iran and Iraq, the southern cone of Africa and Namibian independence, and the reduction of middle-range and even tactical and strategic missiles':

A climate of *detente* means reduced military spending, a prerequisite for freeing the financial flows to solve the debt problem and giving decisive aid of the kind needed by developing countries without affecting the living standards the people of the developed world have today. To take this a step further, it can also be argued that this is important in the current world crisis as it will help revive the developed economies today facing a lack of markets. It is not that the markets are not there. Peoples that would like to buy cannot because they do not have the money. It is a mutual economic crisis, and one way to benefit workers in the US, Britain, or anywhere else in the developed world is to increase the purchasing power of Third World countries...
A rallying call for unity, beyond ideological frontiers, is the struggle not to pay the debt and to have a new international economic order. The two are indivisible. The developed capitalist economies have only a quarter of the world's population; we, the other three-quarters, have been marginalised.

Mass organisations, as well as government in Cuba, have been campaigning hard on the debt question, in such a way that most Cubans have by now a relatively sophisticated analysis of the issue. They might not be familiar with every detail and technicality, but will be able to argue the general principles. They know how the Third World debt has been accrued, what it has been spent on and for whose benefit; and they know how Western banks and bankers have prospered and are now making plans to escape from a crisis of their own making. The common perception of the IMF is as an inventor

The Debt Game

'Deuda Eterna' (Eternal Debt), a pun on 'Deuda Externa' (Foreign Debt) is the name of a Cuban board game. A Third World equivalent of 'Monopoly', all the players are pitted against the banker, the IMF. The starting point is Latin America, and in the centre of the board are South and North. Most of the numbered spaces represent raw materials from the South or manufactured goods from the North. Players landing on the latter must buy from the IMF at high prices. Those landing on the former may sell to the IMF for small sums, but may also buy the land, whereupon other players landing there must pay them, not the banker. Industries purchased (from the IMF) for the Sugar square, for example, come at a high price and borrowing is at a ten per cent interest rate each time round the board.

Forfeit spaces include Flight of Capital, Protectionist Tariffs, Military Coups, IMF Conditions and 12 October 1492, each of which can wipe out some, if not all, of the player's gold and cash reserves and lead to the debt trap. No matter how little money they need, players must borrow in increments of US$1,000 and when they owe US$10,000 are required to throw three instead of two dice (at US$20,000, four dice) for each turn, therefore going round the board faster and having to pay more interest.

Victory over the IMF requires owning the 12 South properties and three national and three export industries corresponding to each. Then the player can refuse to pay the debt and be declared winner. But this is virtually impossible for a single player; hence, the teaming up mechanisms. The board has four Solidarity spaces, where players take a card from a central stack: 'Peru gives you a fishing boat worth US$3,200','El Salvador gives each player US$2,000 for its liberation struggle'... On the Nationalisation space, a player can choose an unowned property and receive with it one free industry. Falling on the Don't Pay space means not having to pay interest on that turn round the board and is where players can form a Debtors Club. On the Latin America space, players can enter into any kind of agreement.

An IMF trump card consists of black boots on Marine-occupied IMF boxes, but Solidarity Card No. 2 is Sandino's Hat which can wipe them out.

of adjustment programmes, watchdog and international alibi for those who hold financial power, and of rescheduling as a euphemism for borrowing new money in order to service old loans.

The Cuban government position was spelt out by Vice-President Carlos Rafael Rodríguez to the May 1988 Third World Foundation Debt Conference: 'It is both immoral and a political mistake to

115

attempt to pay the debt, because it throws governments into greater and greater contradiction with their peoples, who end up suffering the consequences of a debt they did not contract'. A joint stand by the countries of Latin America, one of the world's biggest debtor regions, he argued, could have relevance for Africa and other parts of the world:

> Nobody is out to bankrupt the international financial system. When Cuba postulated that the debt was unpayable, it outlined formulas that would enable banks to assimilate debtors' non-payments. We are now closer than ever to that possibility, given the prospects for eliminating the nuclear weapons that threatened our very existence and since a complete general disarmament is no longer an unrealisable dream. Money that today goes on war could tomorrow go on development; putting an end to the debt burden is no utopia, for each year, equivalent sums go into preparing for world holocaust... All this is but part of a wider project. Not paying the debt is not enough. With continuing unequal exchange, monetary disequilibrium and high interest rates, the debt will again be a problem for us... A change in the international scenario, the establishment of a new economic order to correct those imbalances, is a *sine qua non* for the elimination of the debt, contributing not only to countries' economic development, but also to a new relationship between the underdeveloped world and the more developed industrialised countries with stagnating markets, unemployment and minimal growth... In the same way as solutions are being found for military confrontation, it is high time we put an end to that other confrontation in which hundreds of millions find themselves subject to poverty and backwardness, even in economies that have the capacity to prosper.

Cuba sees peace as a prerequisite for development, and development as a prerequisite for peace. It condemns the idea of military supremacy dominating world politics, and is alert to the fact that regional conflicts are to a certain degree the reflection of global contradictions. 'We cannot be terrified, passive spectators; we must be active fighters in the struggle for peace in the world', Rodríguez declared to the Non-Aligned Coordinating Bureau. How, he also asked, can small Third World countries living under threat disarm themselves and therefore jeopardise their right to self-defence? Cuba in the 1980s had a conventional defence and militia capacity to deflect any threat to its sovereignty. The USSR had aided in building up its capacity, just as Cuba subsequently helped Angola, and in smaller ways Nicaragua. Such issues of Third World sovereignty continued to be crucial to any lasting peace settlement. Nonetheless, the progressive reduction of arms, especially nuclear arms, starting with

116

the big powers, was an essential precondition to progress. Then, he argued, as the threat of military catastrophe recedes, a first step to ending economic catastrophe could be a debtors' club of Third World countries, a desperately needed response of unity to counter First World creditors' clubs. Such reasoning has not fallen on deaf ears.

5. Looking West

Development is commonly equated with change. The term carries with it various expectations of progress for society. However, perceptions of the prospects for and nature of development, as well as the means by which it can be achieved, differ enormously. Not least, such perceptions and resulting action have to function in response to conditions in the real world, and change over time. This can be observed, for instance, in differing priorities for national strategies and policies in the context of Latin America and the Western Hemisphere, of which Cuba is firmly a part.

Out of the 1930s there emerged an expressed need for greater state intervention in managing the economy and society, with calls for greater social equity and minimum state welfare provisions. In the aftermath of the Second World War, this blossomed into the notion of the developmental state as a stimulant and organiser of socio-economic modernisation. A concept that cut across geographical and ideological divides, it was one that in Latin America was generally situated up until the 1950s within the capitalist reform model. The first successful socialist challenge came in 1959 with the Cuban revolution, followed two decades later by revolutions in Grenada and Nicaragua (1979), and interludes such as the 1970-73 Popular Unity government in Chile in between. The rationale of these radical projects hinged on the need for the state to take over and redistribute national wealth through land reform and nationalisation in order to generate the finance for large-scale, state-run development programmes and massive welfare spending, aimed at eliminating inequalities, poverty and disease.

The net effect was to introduce a new dimension into the Latin American development debate. In the mainstream approaches of the 1960s, this ranged from greater national commitment to the reform model of the Alliance for Progress (largely to avert another Cuba)

119

to pressures from within ECLA for a restructuring of Latin American development processes. The former, a US-backed initiative, was dressed in the garb of redistribution with growth and basic needs approaches (state guarantees for minimum personal consumption levels of food, shelter, clothing, plus provision of public services, health, sanitation and education). The latter explicitly rejected prevailing 'Western' development philosophy and the inequities it had continued to generate, and put on the world agenda notions of unequal exchange and the increasing polarity between the industrialised nations (the centre) and less developed agricultural nations (the periphery). Out of a weakness in the Latin American structuralist approach, namely, the internal, national dimension, grew a whole body of dependency theory to explain domestic economic, social and political structures in 'periphery' countries. It also produced the call for a new international economic order which was to be endorsed by the UN, and the more recent critique of the foreign debt phenomenon as a flow of resources from the underdeveloped world to the developed world, and not *vice-versa*.

Structuralist and dependency approaches attacked the notion that international economic and political relations were fundamentally sound and that domestic mismanagement was the root cause of underdevelopment. Socialist approaches focused on the domestic order, but coincided in their analysis of the international structures which exerted a continued, albeit buffered, pressure on their economies and societies. Indeed, nascent socialist states faced formidable political and economic odds in their attempt to modernise in a way that narrowed, rather than exacerbated, the class and urban/rural divide, so as to introduce greater equity and welfare provision for the whole population.

The unforeseen new element in the Latin American, and global, context in the 1980s has been what is now called the disaggregation or 'rolling-back' of the state. One of the early powerful arguments for the developmental state, especially in a post-colonial Third World context, was the perceived need to develop quickly, to 'catch up', to regulate market forces to national advantage. Similarly, the growth of the 'welfare state' was very much a response to the inequities of market forces, a need to regulate for the social good. Today, the concern is with states regulating badly or, in more extreme cases, not being able to regulate at all. States have created cumbersome bureaucracies and new elites acting in their own interests; across the political spectrum, they have often been wasteful, undynamic, inflexible and authoritarian, if not absolutist, repressive and corrupt. New notions of the need to strike a balance between the parametric (minimal) and pervasive (maximal) state have raised lively debate as to the historical circumstance when either can and needs to play a role, and when such a state can outlive its historical welcome. Where the state should end and civil society begin, where market forces might be not only necessary but desirable, and where individual responsibilities lie are issues again cutting across ideological divides and raising new imponderables as to national equity and welfare initiatives.

Recent thinking has extrapolated the argument to look at the state in Third World peripheral socialist economies. Early socialist development models saw industrialisation and modernisation as the road to self-suffiency and capital accumulation, with heavy centralised planning. The newer waves of smaller Third World socialist revolutions have had to seek accumulation through export agriculture for foreign exchange, both of which are far less susceptible to state planning and controls. This has constituted a powerful argument for greater flexibility and decentralisation. However, in small vulnerable states, effective economic planning and development have been rendered more difficult by economic blockade and politico-military hostility on the part of vested foreign interests. Thus, it might equally be argued that, given the levels of vulnerability and hostility, sheer survival has made a strong centralised leadership and controls crucial. The resultant balancing of such contradictory pushes and pulls has been possibly the major development factor, and is one that in the Americas the US has tried to manipulate to its advantage in the context of Cuba, Grenada and Nicaragua.

In the case of Cuba, within the constraints of mono-crop export agriculture, the country did at the time of the revolution have a sizeable industrial base, and modernisation through industrialisation (whether heavy or light) has been a continued goal. And yet it is the one objective that has perhaps been most blocked through a variety of factors, not least the external limitations of the global political economy. It is the economic, political, military and intelligence interplay of those limitations that will be in focus here, the emphasis being on that centre of political power: the US/West.

Confrontation and Cooperation

Given the tight integration of Cuba's pre-revolutionary agro-industrial economy into that of the US, the young revolution was bound to be highly vulnerable to US-spearheaded external pressures. This was always taken into account in discussions of problems in the

121

early revolutionary period, though arguably not in its true dimension. Moreover, as time passed and Cuba became more integrated into the socialist bloc, this factor was deemed less and less important. The notion of the 'war economy' has been all too often dismissed as a political convenience of the Cubans to explain away domestic inadequacies, especially in the present day. The truth in its entirety lies neither with the conspiracy theory of history nor with mismanagement on the home front. But the fact of the matter is that successive US administrations have up to the present used differing combinations of coercive economic, political, ideological, military and intelligence levers, in bilateral, regional and global arenas, in an attempt to bring Cuba to its knees. They have pushed Cuba along paths that might otherwise never have been taken and have continually undermined its growing achievements, both at home and abroad. Cuban and overseas analysts now suggest that, rather than having a decreasing effect on domestic progress, these adverse pressures may today be more crucial to Cuba than ever, as greater levels of development demand greater levels of global integration, with both West and East, if further development is not to be obstructed.

Early economic plans based on a complementary programme of agricultural and industrial development were intended to maintain sugar production and foreign exchange earnings, while lowering the demand for food imports and industrial raw materials. Poor economic performance, which led to the balance of payments crisis of 1963 and the reversion to an emphasis on agriculture, was certainly in part due to the tension and disorganisation of large-scale structural change. Nonetheless, two major points are important. Firstly, the very real threat of external military intervention and legitimate concern for national security caused scarce financial and physical resources to be diverted to defence. After 1959, armed forces and reserves expanded twelve-fold from 50,000 to 600,000, costing a sum estimated to be over ten per cent of the new national budget in 1963. US-backed paramilitary expeditions (invasion in the case of the Bay of Pigs or Playa Girón) and the sabotage and espionage operations of the 1960s brought into being a Cuban military-intelligence-civil defence industry that made the trade blockade a greater strain than it might otherwise have been. Secondly, the extent to which the government simply could not obtain basic industrial equipment, spare parts and materials from traditional US markets, was extremely damaging to overall production levels and contributed to the foreclosure of rapid heavy industrial development. Then, for the rest of the sugar-dominated 1960s, breakdowns and malfunctioning of

US-made sugar mill machinery caused by shortages of spare parts were a constant problem.

The shift to the socialist bloc for export markets and supply sources posed new problems for economic efficiency, namely integrating socialist bloc machinery into US- and Western European-built plants. Vehicles and tractors did not function in the tropical climate; spare parts were often costly and of inferior quality; imports could not keep pace with breakdowns, and, when procured in the West by the Soviet Union for trans-shipment to Cuba, costs multiplied and increased the pressure on Cuba's low foreign exchange reserves. Again, in those early years the transportation blockade, causing Cuba to look to more distant markets, was estimated to have tripled shipping costs. It also created the need for shipyards, repair facilities and warehouses to handle cost-effective bulk shipping consignments from the Soviet Union and Eastern Europe. The dilemmas are all too familiar today, with the current spare parts problem for equipment and machinery, and transport and shipping bottlenecks that put serious strains on the Havana bus network and brought Havana docks almost to a standstill in the summer of 1988.

US measures to drive a hostile politico-military bargain with an unaccommodating neighbour, to effectively isolate and blockade Cuba in the West, have acted as a powerful constraint on the developing socialist economy, contributing to the perpetuation of monoculture and external vulnerability and thereby curbing the national effort to transform economy and society. In the case of the blockade, it is interesting that official US reports continue to argue for the embargo as a major barrier to Cuba's development effort. A 1982 study entitled 'Cuba faces the economic realities of the 1980s', prepared for the Joint Economic Committee of the US Congress, was chillingly accurate in some, if not all, of its forecasts for Cuba by the mid-decade. A detailed study of the centrality of foreign trade to the island's development, it stated bluntly:

> The US embargo has been and continues to be not only a major, but a crucial impediment to Cuba's efforts at diversifying and expanding its hard currency trade, the key to improved growth and living standards... [COMECON] aid may continue to protect the Cuban revolution from economic disaster, but only just. For the average Cuban, the outlook is for more austerity — perhaps interrupted by small periodic advances when the sugar price swings upward. On the other hand, if shortfalls occur in Soviet energy supplies, an austerity scenario will prove to be the best outcome Havana can anticipate.

As an analysis of some of the obvious economic issues, it is worth considering the report in more detail. It began with a revolutionary balance sheet:

> On his 54th birthday in 1980, Fidel Castro could reflect on twenty years of unique social experiment in the Western Hemisphere. At the outset, the Cuban revolution gathered widespread support from most of the population with the promise of both an improved living standard and a new pride of nationalism... After two decades, a comprehensive assessment of the Cuban economy is especially timely. First, Cuba's development model has attracted admiration in the Third World as having 'solved' the multifaceted social, economic, and political problems of development. Second, Cuba has probably exhausted the gains as perceived by the population from the installation of socialist egalitarianism and has become more and more deeply involved in and dependent on trade with and subsidies from far distant economies. Havana therefore faces crucial economic decisions in the next half decade which will set development prospects long into the future, including, probably the post-Castro generation.

The genuine socio-economic and political accomplishments of the revolution that were cited as attracting international attention included: a highly egalitarian distribution of income that has eliminated malnutrition, especially among children; the establishment of a national health care programme that rivals that of numerous developed countries; the near total elimination of illiteracy and a highly developed multilevel educational system; and a relatively well disciplined and motivated population with a strong sense of national identity.

While these achievements were noted as significant and distinctive among LDCs (the World Bank acronym for less developed countries), it was postulated that they had entailed substantial costs. Cuba's reliance on a centrally planned economy and controlled society was held to have resulted in systemic economic inefficiency and political conflicts abroad that had necessitated continuous massive economic and military aid from the USSR. Notwithstanding what the report calculated at US$13,000 million in Soviet aid over the last decade, poor economic performance was seen as evidenced by: dependence on maximum Soviet aid to meet minimum investment and consumption needs; real economic growth barely exceeding population growth; continued extreme dependence on sugar; stagnating living standards, an oppressively inefficient bureaucracy and poor labour productivity; heavy reliance on COMECON trade, where supply constraints and delivery problems severely compound economic management difficulties; and near total reliance on a single energy source, as Soviet exports were providing 98 per cent of Cuba's oil and three-fourths of its total energy needs.

Some of the revolution's accomplishments, it was argued, had themselves generated adverse economic consequences which were causing Havana increasing difficulties: the institutionalisation of a Soviet-type centrally planned economy had burdened Cuba with a vast administrative bureaucracy that stifled innovation, productivity and efficiency necessary for economic advance; the agriculturally dominated economy would be hard pressed to find employment for a highly educated labour force that was growing by three per cent annually; centralised management of foreign trade had been difficult given Cuba's low profile in COMECON and its inflexibility in responding to import requirements not in the plan; continual austerity and the sacrifice of consumerism had created popular discontent; the egalitarian distribution of income had eroded material incentives and dissipated labour motivation; and Cuba's 'aggressive international profile', emphasising identification with 'violent' revolutionary struggle in the Third World and its close association with Soviet foreign policy objectives, 'had prejudiced relations with the US and other Western countries, such that the US trade embargo had continued to restrict Havana's economic development options, necessitating an ever growing dependence on COMECON, especially the USSR'.

The US is skilled at producing blends of untruths, half-truths and home truths. The 1982 study was calculated to propagate the 'new dependency' theory of patron-client relations, with Cuba as the client state of the USSR, and to perpetuate the blockade as what it has always been: a hard economic attempt to take political measures against Cuba. It amasses significant amounts of data on Soviet economic assistance and prospects for COMECON integration, much of which is only questionable in terms of interpretation. Four key areas are worthy of further analysis.

First, the role of foreign trade in Cuban economic development can hardly be overemphasised. Prior to the revolution, 75 per cent of exports and 65 percent of imports were in trade with the US. Twenty years later, COMECON countries accounted for some 75 per cent (today 85 per cent) of foreign trade, with the USSR by far in the lead. Cuban trade within COMECON essentially involves a barter exchange of sugar, nickel, citrus and other products in return for raw materials, industrial equipment, and some consumer products, including food, according to pre-arranged annual plans and prices. Cuba fits into the COMECON principle of 'international specialisation'.

Second, despite the COMECON/USSR predominance, an essential portion of Cuban trade has been with the West. This dropped from 40 per cent in the mid-1970s, 25-30 percent in 1982, to 15 per cent in 1988. The drop reflects more a curtailment of previous levels of Western trading, rather than any switch to the East, since commerce from the two is largely complementary. Neither is the drop in volume altogether commensurate with value, as fluctuating commodity prices mean that Cuba can buy less for the same amount of hard currency.

Third, among the reasons for the importance of certain hard currency exports are: although there has been a steady decline in the share of food products in total imports, from 20.5 per cent in 1958 to 9.3 per cent in 1986, 30-35 per cent of Cuban foodstuffs are still imported and many of these are unavailable or in short supply in COMECON; many of the quality consumer goods important for labour productivity are obtainable only in hard currency, as again COMECON countries have no great expertise in consumer areas; technology and machinery in COMECON countries are often lacking (partly because of similar blockade and currency difficulties to the ones Cuba has faced); and the current debt must be serviced. In the uneven pricing structure of the West, Cuban efforts to maintain minimum imports from hard currency countries, including chemicals, industrial inputs, machinery and consumer goods have resulted in large trade deficits and growing debt, from US$1,000 million in 1974, US$26,000 million in 1980, to US$62,000 million in 1988. With access to new credits limited, hard currency resources for the foreseeable future appear to be restricted to earnings on exports to the West, income from tourism, and Soviet hard currency aid.

Fourth, foreign trade deficiencies have both resulted from and contributed to domestic economic difficulties. In the 1976-80 five-year period, performance fell short of plan. This caused the second 1981-5 plan to be less ambitious on targets, with express goals including export expansion and import substitution to reduce trade dependence, and greater emphasis on people's needs such as *per capita* income, caloric intake, housing construction and electrification.

The 1982 US conclusion was as follows:

> After 20 years of social and economic experimentation, the Cuban revolution now appears to confront a most uncertain period for sustaining its achievements. Cuba is still burdened with many of the rigid controls of a command economy modeled on the Soviet system and tied to Moscow by massive subsidies. In addition, Havana faces unprecedented economic pressures in the areas of energy, productivity

and unemployment... In past crises Soviet largesse has always been available to offset failures and defuse pressures for any substantial change in the system, but Cuba may be less fortunate in the 1980s, as its continuing economic difficulties may coincide with a leveling off of Soviet assistance forced by competing demands from other allies.

The key 'aid', or 'subsidy', from the USSR and other COMECON countries comes, of course, in the form of trade prices that are heavily favourable to Cuba, particularly the sugar/oil exchange. The fact that the 'subsidy' was seen to rise so much in the 1970s was due to the newly depressed sugar and inflated oil prices on the residual 'free' capitalist world market. Thus, in 1979, Moscow was paying five times the going sugar price and selling its oil at one-third the OPEC rate. At the same time, this was augmented by Soviet hard currency purchases of sugar at going world market prices, to the tune of one-sixth of Cuba's hard currency earnings. Developments in the 1980s involved intricate arrangements whereby Cuba began to buy sugar at the new low world market price to resell to the USSR, and, whereas Cuba had before been reselling oil abroad at high prices, the USSR sought new lower-price oil deals with Venezuela to freight oil to Cuba, to help undercut massive shipping costs. Written into the 1986-90 Soviet-Cuban trade agreement was also a provision to the effect that the fraction of the Soviet/Cuba oil trade yielding hard currency revenue would increase if Cuba could cut real fuel imports below levels scheduled. This was a powerful incentive to step up conversion of sugar waste or bagasse into an oil substitute, and thereby free the USSR to sell elsewhere the oil it is not obliged to deliver to Cuba.

Viewed in the macro-economic terms of the US study, even the 1979 US$3,000 million figure of aid equalled only 0.4 per cent of Soviet GDP, and Soviet oil deliveries to Cuba, only two per cent of Soviet oil production and 13 per cent of Soviet exports to COMECON. The hard currency cost was more significant, amounting to some six per cent of potential earnings, especially when the USSR was reliant on oil for almost one-half of its hard currency earnings, and when there was also increasing demand from other COMECON allies, some of them new (Vietnam and Ethiopia, for example). This helps to explain why the USSR and Cuba place high hopes on a joint nuclear energy programme on the island, as well as smaller-scale harnessing of fuel from cane bagasse, sun, water and wind.

Interestingly, Cuba, the USSR and the US all seem to agree on Cuba's key economic priorities: to diversify access to energy resources, diversify the production base away from sugar and expand hard-currency exports, reduce the debt burden, improve efficiency and productivity of the domestic economy, and improve popular living standards. The differences of political perspective are that the US sees these objectives as possible only if Cuba comes more into the Western fold, on US terms. This would mean Cuba compromising some hard political principles, nationally and internationally, which it is clearly unprepared to do. The Soviet bloc has not always been as ready as Cuba to put these principles into action in Third World contexts, values greater *detente* with the US, and would like to see more internal efficiency in Cuba, but has not itself always been an example of productive efficiency. Cuba has its own criticisms, not only concerning shortfalls of deliveries, but also the variety and quality of products available from the USSR/COMECON, which make satisfying consumer needs and boosting worker productivity difficult. Given the extent of growing irritation in COMECON countries also over precisely such consumer areas, it is difficult to see how COMECON can help much in this regard.

Cuban planners have to manage importing and exporting according to pre-set targets and an annual trade plan, on the basis of two very different foreign trade markets, each with its own problems. On the one hand, there is COMECON trade with its built-in rigidity and inefficiency. On the other, lies the hard currency trade, where rapid changes in commodity markets demand rapid responses to make the most efficient use of scarce resources. Dealing with both markets simultaneously can cause expensive mistakes for trading enterprises and for the internal economy dependent on them. One example on the 'free' market was the short-sighted anticipation of continued high sugar earnings in 1975-6, and subsequently high oil re-export earnings, whereby Cuba took on seriously over-extended commitments for hard currency imports, leading to contract cancellation and disruption of trade flows.

Washington's policy is to try to keep up the pressure on Cuba, as on the socialist camp in general, in the hope of forcing collapse or change. The greatest US hope is that what collapses will be national unity, that there will be internal strife, as has happened when the strain has been too great for other socialist countries. One spark to Polish discontent was the reported discovery of canned meat products destined for Cuba, disguised under fake labels as non-meat items. There were rumours of a labour dispute in Havana's docks over a shipment of buses to Nicaragua in late 1988. The parallels are obvious, but it would be hard to categorise either as political opposition to domestic or international socialism *per se*.

Vendetta Politics

The pursuit of 'vendetta politics' is how Morris Morley describes US attitudes towards Cuba in his book *Imperial State and Revolution*. The study charts how the US swiftly developed a confrontational approach, attempting to work initially through inside groups hostile to the new regime and then increasingly from the outside through public and clandestine strategies, overt and covert war on both political and economic fronts. It focuses at length on the effectiveness of economic sanctions for political goals during the 1964-8 Johnson era, when none of Cuba's major capitalist trading partners made any great attempt to challenge Washington, though moderate trade was maintained with Havana. It recounts how, for example, Britain was a target for US pressure from the early 1960s, because of its continuing trade ties with Cuba. The British Leyland contract for buses, spare parts, repair shops and credits, the company's largest in years, was a particular source of concern. The deal went through, but the US managed to discourage British ships from transporting the buses, and one East German vessel laden with buses was rammed in the Thames. Other forms of economic sabotage included untraceable chemical additives in lubricants for Cuban diesel engines to make them wear out faster and asymmetrical ball bearings which would damage Cuban machines.

In his treatment of the Nixon, Ford and Carter administrations, Morley highlights the multiplicity of attitudes within the US corporate and business community regarding the profitable normalisation of economies ties with Cuba, along with governmental insistence that any changes in bilateral relations be dependent on Cuban concessions, especially in the area of foreign policy and external alignments. Cuban support for Third World nationalist and socialist revolutions ran counter to the primary expressed goal of all post-Second World War administrations: to keep open as much of the world economy as possible to foreign capital. Carter shifted more to an interventionist foreign policy late in his presidency, before Reagan oversaw an extraordinary intensification of US military, strategic and covert capabilities, to reassert US military superiority over the USSR, limit the ability of the Western Alliance (Western Europe and Japan) to pursue independent economic and foreign policies, and reverse established revolutionary governments in the Third World. This was accompanied by a vast expansion of CIA paramilitary assets and an intelligence budget that grew at a faster rate than the defence budget between 1981 and 1985.

The Reagan administration simply saw the need to get tough with Cuba, and, in the context of developments in Central America and the Caribbean, a military response was never totally excluded. The US military build-up in Central America, including a series of naval and military manoeuvres of unprecedented scope, was also designed to intimidate Havana, described in 1981 by Vice-President Bush and Secretary of State Haig as 'the principal threat to peace in the region'. The US build-up caused Cuba in turn to strengthen its military capabilities. Soviet military aid to Cuba is estimated to have at least doubled over 1980-81, and since then to have been maintained at the 1981 level. Cuba in addition organised a new militia of 500,000 to supplement the regular army should Reagan have pursued the military option. However, an always limited and, since 1982, apparently declining Cuban military presence in Central America contrasted with US escalation.

Other Pentagon/CIA plans, some envisaged, some carried out, have included a naval quarantine to block oil supplies and covert action against Cuban supply lines and Cubans in, for example, Nicaragua, where schools and health centres staffed by substantial numbers of Cubans have been either destroyed or forced to close down. The 1982 US National Security Council covert action programme summed it up: 'we have a vital interest in not allowing the proliferation of Cuba-model states'. US intransigence was such that any diplomacy was played down, and all but a few of the repeated overtures from the Cubans for bilateral talks, whether on immigration or foreign policy, especially Central America and southern Africa, were turned down.

It was clear that, beyond the proliferation argument, lay the larger objectives of undermining the Cuban revolution, breaking Havana's economic and military alliance with the USSR and tightening the global blockade to reduce the country's access to hard currency earnings. In 1982, the few remaining US-Cuban bilateral economic links were targeted for partial repeal or complete removal. The Trading with the Enemy act added stringent financial restrictions to the pre-Carter travel ban, effectively putting a stop to all US tourist and business travel to the island.

The Reagan administration's economic offensive, however, centred on three major areas: sabotaging or obstructing Cuba's debt negotiations with Western creditors; denying Havana access to capitalist sources of financing; and pressuring allies not to sell merchandise or purchase goods from the island. In 1981 it secured a cancellation of a loan through the French state-owned bank Credit Lyonnais. A US trading prohibition was put on over 40 'pass-through' companies in Latin America and Europe for US machinery, parts and other goods. US export privileges were withdrawn for Western companies such as the Spanish Piher and Japanese Toshiba known to be trading with Havana. The US trading ban on the French Creusot Loire steel company was only lifted in 1981 after the French government certified it was no longer using nickel imports from Cuba. It was also US pressure that led to the collapse of Canadian-Cuban projects for off-shore oil exploration and citrus processing. The cumulative effect in lost trade and investment was to force Cuba to renegotiate on credits, and lose it its no-risk reputation among Western financial circles, whereupon the State Department mobilised to discredit Cuban economic reports to creditors and ensure that there would be no special rescheduling treatment.

Washington was only partially successful, however, as Western confidence in Cuba was not mistakenly anchored in the belief that Soviet and COMECON commitment would obviate any serious threat to the island economy. Contrary to US predictions, and even with the unforeseen developments of *perestroika*, *glasnost* and *detente*, the new 1986-90 COMECON agreements were on even more favourable terms for the island: a 50 per cent increase in Soviet aid over the previous five-year pact, and a commitment to reschedule all Cuba's debt payments to Socialist bloc countries falling due before 1990, and to help Cuba with its Western creditors.

Europe and Latin America: Alternative Markets

In May 1985, Cuban officials were arguing on the basis of economic growth that the economy was capable of export expansion, but needed the cooperation of its capitalist trading partners. In April 1986, the unusually poor sugar harvest, low world sugar prices and the collapse of oil prices forced massive rescheduling of the debt, and in July a critical hard currency shortage forced Cuba to stop payment on both principal and interest, pending meetings with public and private creditors. On the financial, as well as the trading front, French, Spanish, British and other Western commercial circles have engaged in only limited accommodation to Washington, and have continued to base their decisions on more pragmatic business considerations.

There have, however, been considerable differences between official government positions, as taken by Thatcher in Britain and González in Spain. By 1985 Cuba had become Spain's most important Latin American market and a US$62 million Spanish-government guaranteed credit was to facilitate exports to Cuba. Whitehall, on the other hand, strictly limits the amount of state credit guarantees (up until 1985, two credit insurance facilities of £5 million each) available in any one year, and has imposed stringent conditions on exporters' access to this assistance. This has been repeatedly criticised by the Confederation of British Industry. A major boost came in 1985, with a £30 million credit line from Midland Bank, and in 1986 with a unique five-year agreement between the US private-sector trading company Goodwood, backed by Midland, and a socialist state trading agency, aimed at increasing bilateral trade over the period by £350 million. The company will purchase £40 million worth of Cuban exports annually, while Havana will import £30 million in British goods. As the *Financial Times* reported at the time, one factor stimulating British trade interest was the attraction of doing business in the US 'back yard' without having to compete with US companies.

If its Western allies are not always submissive to US pressure, a new international scenario of considerable dimensions has been unfolding in Latin America since 1982. Arguably, Britain acted as a catalyst in this respect, when the Falklands/Malvinas War created the possibility of continent-wide political re-alignment on the basis of nationalist and anti-imperialist issues. This was greatly aided by the post-1983 collapse of authoritarian military regimes and redemocratisation processes in strategically important countries such as Argentina and Brazil, a more regional approach to problems like the foreign debt and a renewed perception of the US as a critical part of those problems. Prior to this, there had been a deterioration in Cuban relations with Venezuela, Jamaica, Costa Rica, Colombia, Panama and Peru. Only Mexico had continued its ties and, in January 1981, signed two major economic agreements: the state oil company was to assist with off-shore oil exploration and modernisation of refineries, and Mexico was to purchase 100,000 tons of sugar. Half a year later, however, Washington forced Mexico's complicity and excluded Cuba from the North-South summit in Cancún. By 1985, Argentina had surpassed Mexico as the principal Latin American exporter to Cuba, with government-backed credit lines envisaging trade worth up to US$300 million a year.

Brazil-Cuba relations had begun to thaw even in the late 1970s under the generals, and the 1979 Figueiredo government lifted restrictions in several areas, including travel, culture, sport and business. Consultation in regional organisations such as GLACSEC (the Group of Latin American and Caribbean Sugar Exporting Countries) became the norm rather than the exception. By 1982, Brazilian businessmen were convinced that Cuba was a potential market for at least US$200 million worth of Brazilian goods. The

Cubans were particularly interested in machinery and equipment used in the production of sugar and fuel alcohol from cane, in which Brazilian technology was every bit as advanced as that of the US. Since the direct sale of Brazilian exports to Cuba was illegal, complicated triangular arrangements involved third countries: by 1986, exports via Mexico, Panama, Argentina and Venezuela totalled between US$8 and 10 million, and helped the push towards normalised diplomatic relations in 1986. That same year, Brazil and Cuba held bilateral meetings to work out a common strategy to force the US (and the European Economic Community) to end their restrictions on sugar imports from Latin America and the Caribbean. Their action followed an October meeting of GLACSEC at which the entire membership walked out in support of Cuba after the US delegate accused the Castro government of unfair trade practices!

Of all the Latin American governments, Colombia has played perhaps the most surprising role, with Belisario Betancur courting Castro both personally, and through the Third World's non-aligned movement and Latin America's Contadora Group effort for a Central America peace settlement. Colombia has been in the forefront to hasten Cuba's readmission to the Organisation of American States (OAS), from which it was expelled in 1962, although the US position has so far prevailed. It was also Colombia that tabled the motion at the 1988 UN Human Rights Commission in Geneva, whereby Cuba was given the floor to invite a commission of enquiry to investigate US allegations against Cuba.

New Peace, Trade Wars and Blocs: the EEC, COMECON and Cuba

New thinking in Europe recognises that military power has not prevented the US from becoming the world's biggest debtor, a country whose economy now depends on Japanese and European funding of the Federal deficit. Similarly, Soviet bloc military power has been achieved at the cost of an economy now dependent on loans and investments from weaker but richer neighbours. (Collectively, the bloc owes more than the record Latin American debtor Brazil. Food shortages, mounting debt and internal stabilisation through military power have led to the so-called Africanisation of Eastern Europe.) Sagging US and Soviet economies mean that the arms race is over, it is argued. The real winners of the Cold War, moreover, are those who have spent least on it: Japan and Western Europe, military pygmies but economic giants. Japan is already playing a growing role in Latin America and other Third World countries, whether in the form of business ventures, trading agreements or credit financing, and Cuba is likely to be no exception. 'Fortress Europe' is how the new European Community of 1992 has been described. Even so, economic realities can hardly be so neatly encapsulated. With 36 per cent of the London international banking business in Japanese hands, Japan is one country set to do well out of 1992. Similarly, economic trends well into 1988 showed how Britain, for example, spent US$16,080 million buying assets in the US and US$2,975 million in the EEC. A parallel 40 per cent of current US overseas investment is in the EEC, and must modify West European protectionism. More significantly, however, during 1988 there were extended loans and credits in the order of US$10,000 million to Gorbachev's USSR, and talk of a new Marshall Plan to rebuild Eastern Europe. The Spanish Socialist Party's 'Programme 2000' sees Eastern Europe playing the same kind of role for the EEC that Southern Europe played to the North in the 1960s and 1970s: economies that in the process of growth then become valuable markets (and perhaps overtake, one might add, like Italy now surpassing Britain in economic indicators).

The June 1988 agreement between the European Economic Community and COMECON was a breakthrough in East-West relations, establishing a new European trading structure after nearly two decades of negotiations. Though commercial agreements are to be negotiated bilaterally between individual EEC and COMECON countries, the Common Declaration provided the official basis for them. The EEC aside, it has potentially important economic and political implications for all the countries of Eastern Europe and their three developing world partners, Vietnam, Mongolia and Cuba. Officials in Havana certainly see the agreement as opening the way for crucial discussions with the EEC on finance and trade, especially regarding negotiations for a new international sugar trade agreement and in areas such as machinery and plant production in sugar, sugar by-products and health. Cuba is optimistic that, as a Latin American country with membership of both COMECON and the non-aligned movement, it is in a strong position to take advantage of the new agreement. Since diplomatic relations have been established with the EEC, it can participate in the Latin American Group in Brussels.

In the wake of the agreement, the London-based *Cuba Business* magazine pointed out that previous amounts of financial aid and other assistance to Cuba had been small: only US$13.2 million out of total EEC official development assistance to Latin America of US$678.3 million, over the period 1979-85. Official development assistance from individual countries had been negligible. Net receipts from individual EEC countries amounted to US$163.2 million during 1980-85, compared to US$28,941 million for Latin America as a whole. Nearly all of this aid was from France and Italy, with hardly any from the UK.

One bone of contention as regards increased assistance and trading will have to be terms, prices and the impact of the EEC's Common Agricultural Policy (CAP) on the world sugar market. The massive growth in productivity and output in European agriculture as a result of EEC subsidies since the early 1970s led first to a reduction of imports and then to the EEC becoming a major agricultural exporter. This displaced other suppliers and caused dramatic price falls, and EEC sugar exports were a major contributor to the 1985 world sugar price slump to three cents per pound, compared with average cane sugar production costs of around 15 cents per pound. Without CAP, it had been estimated that world prices would have been 80 per cent more stable and 7-11 per cent higher, and Third World exporters would have gained US$300 million annually (the main beneficiaries being Cuba, the Philippines, Brazil, the Dominican Republic and Thailand). The lifting of CAP subsidies and the 1988 sugar price high of 16 cents per pound introduces new dimensions which are as yet too early to gauge, but the year 1989 is likely to be important for the future of world agricultural trade, as Europe confronts the US, Japan and the newly industrialised countries, and the newly formed 1986 Cairns Group of agricultural exporters (Australia, Canada, Hungary, New Zealand, Argentina, Brazil and eight other developing countries), as well as COMECON and other blocs in the socialist and developing world.

The late 1980s have brought some interesting developments to those groupings in which Cuba is involved. In April 1988, a new agreement, the first of its kind, to boost mutual trade among under-developed countries was signed at a meeting of 48 countries in Belgrade. It has been called the Global System of Preferential Trade, and under its terms, concessions will be granted by the participating countries on 1,597 products, with special treatment to the least developed exporting countries. Designed to make use of Third World resources and potential, it comes as a timely response to the situation created by the foreign debt and increased protectionism by major capitalist countries. Given the variety of natural resources and different levels of development in differing fields, the idea is that countries can complement each other in goods and in specialist and technical assistance. This initial agreement is small, but could lead to more substantial agreements in the future and contribute to Cuba's diversification strategy. In 1986, Cuba's two-way trade with other Third World countries amounted to only 8.6 percent of its total trade, leaving room for considerable expansion.

Conclusion: Into the Fourth Decade

A vicious circle dictates that Cuba's possibilities for trade with the West and the Third World are drastically affected by reduced availability of hard currency and trade finance and a hard currency debt that is currently rising at an annual rate of 15-20 per cent. Underlying both problems is the continuing *impasse* in negotiations between Cuba and its Western government creditors of the Paris Club and the crisis of the domestic economy. Since Cuba's hard currency debt first emerged as a serious problem at the April 1986 Paris Club meeting (as a result of which US$230 million of the debt was rescheduled), Cuba subsequently failed to meet a number of payments due to governments, public export credit agencies, banks and commercial firms. The July 1987 Paris Club drew attention to 21,000 million pesos in debt maturities falling due, and in 1988 Cuba asked for a rescheduling of capital and interest amounting to US$850 million over 15 years with a grace period of five years. The Paris Club wants Cuba to step up development of the export sector, increase investments in the productive sector and encourage joint ventures (of which there are already a few), at a time when export credit agencies have reduced their commitment to Cuba in response to the problems (exceptions are Spain and Argentina). Some smaller firms engaged in business with Cuba have seen fit to pull out, but other larger companies seem prepared to stay and defer payments for the time being.

Countertrade, or direct barter, offers a possible way out, and a number of such contracts have been signed: a British company supplies 1,200 specially bred pigs in exchange for 6,000 tons of sugar; a Canadian company sells plant for manufacturing egg trays from bagasse in exchange for a proportion of output; Guyana supplies 6,000 tons of rice and 2,000 cubic metres of wood in exchange for 10,000 tons of cement and 5,000 tons of salt.

137

Another hope is to boost trade in non-conventional areas. According to economic indicators, sugar's total share in exports had fallen from 84.5 per cent to 63.9 per cent in 1985. Non-traditional exports (excluding sugar, nickel, tobacco, rum, coffee and oil) that year stood at 18.8 per cent (much more than any other Caribbean nation under the US General System of Preferences and Caribbean Basin Initiative). Between 1980 and 1985, Cuba introduced 111 new export products which included citrus fruits, fish products, steel products, recycled raw materials, scrap metals, paper products, books, cement, fibreboard and other sugar by-products, teletransmission and processing equipment, computer keyboards, and pharmaceutical products. One of the key off-shoots of the health-care system has been a growing medical industry, patenting new technologies and products ranging from external bone fixators and flexor tendon implants to interferon, SUMA HIV detection in Aids, meningitis vaccine and placenta treatment for vitiligo.

The 1985 value of non-sugar exports (excluding oil re-exports) was over 1,000 million pesos, 44 per cent of which was for convertible currency markets. These figures, moreover, do not reflect the rapid growth in tourism; from the 1978 figure of 96,600 foreign tourists visiting the island to the 1985 total of 240,500, four-fifths of whom arrived from the capitalist world. Revenues in 1985 were pegged at US$75 million or 118 million pesos including internal tourist services. In 1986 they rose a further 7.2 per cent, placing tourism ahead of tobacco as Cuba's fourth most important hard currency earner, behind sugar, oil re-exports and fish products. It is estimated to be on its way to second and even first place. The target is to generate over US$400 million a year, cornering 20 per cent of the Caribbean tourism market, but this will require a major transformation of the sector. Hotel occupancy rates are high, in the range of 60-85 per cent over the year, and sold out in the winter season. A major hotel construction programme is under way, envisaging an increase of 60 per cent in hotel rooms by 1992. Currently, only 19 of Havana's 36 hotels are in use, with the remainder either under repair or closed for renovation. Foreign (including US) investment is being sought for joint ventures, contracts have been signed with tour operators in various countries, and a first cruise around Cuba's coastline will be organised by a UK travel company.

Ultimately, these and other kinds of deals depend on the internal economic effort. The Cuban government response of rectification, to root out inefficiency and corruption, and to curtail imports and boost exports, has to be seen in this light. In the first nine months of 1987, it succeeded in increasing exports by 8.8 per cent and reducing hard currency imports by 6.6 per cent. In terms of value, the target for 1987 was to halve the import bill of US$1,200 million to US$600 million, and, in the event it was actually reduced to US$900 million. The growth of hard currency reserves was tagged at four per cent, and reserves on trading with the socialist countries at eight per cent. The overwhelming reduction in the negative Cuban-European trade deficit, from US$500 million in 1985 to US$100 million in late 1988 was not due to increased exports but to the dramatic drop in imports, from US$900 million to US$280 million over the same period. Internally, the Cuban state had saved some 158 million pesos in salaries by cutting back on the payments not in line with labour performance or backed by actual production or services rendered, even when the salaries of agricultural workers and other low-income groups had been raised. However, import cut-backs had been achieved at the cost of significant reductions in imported machinery, equipment and materials that inevitably exacerbated production problems. Gross social product fell by 3.2 per cent, and productivity by just over four per cent in 1987, despite efforts to the contrary.

Mid-1988 figures pointed to an upswing, with figures ranging from seven per cent economic growth in Santiago de Cuba to between four and six per cent growth in other provinces. Among the projects completed were new hospitals, an oil refinery, a pharmaceuticals factory, an electric power station, and tourist development areas. Havana had one of the lowest growth rates (just over four per cent), and seemed to be most beset by a popular mood that was more of an upswing in irritation and downswing in motivation. The mood was due partly to everyday shortages and shortcomings in consumer areas and services, but partly also to a generalised feeling that there had not been enough curtailment of administrative privilege and corruption, and that narrow formulas and empty rhetoric were not altogether adequate responses. The internal tightening up has since produced its own brand of social and economic side-stepping, with new clampdowns on blackmarket dealings, tensions among worker and peasant sectors, rising petty crime rates among less advantaged groups, and growing criticisms that the great new hope of tourism is for the benefit of foreigners only. National tourism has increased greatly over recent years, but excursions, camping trips and second-to-third-class hotels account for much of it. Access to first-and luxury-class hotels is limited to the off-season and prohibitive in the case of dollar area joint-venture beach enclaves. Attempts to improve the level of service, crucial to the tourist business, have included a proposed new law making it possible to sack inefficient workers. An arguably necessary law given the state of the services, it is again one that cannot but generate discontent.

Cuba 30 years on is a blend of tremendous achievements for a Third World country, such that in various indicators, such as health, it is on a par with, if not ahead of, parts of the developed world. Alongside those achievements, there are also growing problems of a social, economic and political kind. In the context of *glasnost* and *perestroika*, there is a growing undercurrent of irregular, but essentially healthy, debate on varying approaches that might be taken within socialist parameters, some of which do not necessarily coincide with current rectification policy. There are also more spontaneous personal reactions to socio-economic and political shortfalls and some public disaffection from certain sectors.

This, Cubans themselves will have to work out. Popular problem-solving ventures involving community initiative have included the Family Doctor programme, microbrigade construction, along with new ventures in rural areas that range from small-scale hydroelectric, solar and wind energy schemes, local service collectives, and direct linking of local marketing to state and cooperative farms. The extent to which initiatives like these can be extended to strained consumer areas, especially in Havana, and go beyond the venting of criticism to more deep-seated changes in the national political arenas probably rests as much on the easing of external as internal pressures.

Intelligence involvements such as the CIA/MI5 incident that led to the expulsion of the Cuban commercial attache and ambassador from Britain serve as reminders of what is least productive in terms of external influence. The true story has yet to emerge, but economic sabotage may well have played its part, in an attempt to check growing commercial and political pressures within both the US and Britain for more normalised relations with Cuba. In 1987, the US Treasury issued 198 licences to US foreign subsidiaries to trade with Cuba, and some Cuban estimates quoted figures of a possible 50 per cent of trade with the West, should the embargo be lifted. From the British perspective, exports to Cuba are important to the Cuban economy and are in the region of £50-80 million a year. Pending at the time of the St John's Wood showdown in September 1988 was the largest British contract ever destined for Cuba, whereby the Cuban shipping line, Mambisa, was looking to British Shipbuilders subsidiary North East Shipbuilders Ltd (NESL) for a £70 million order for ten freighters and a potential part stake in the purchase of NESL's Sunderland yard. The Cuban order and the island's repeated attempts to take work to Sunderland contrasted markedly with the Thatcher government's plans to close the yard.

The political stakes are high, and an effective lobby in the US/West for more equitable relations could go a long way to help normalise relations between Cuba and its traditional antagonists. It is not over-optimistic to assume that the growing process of *detente* and talks between Gorbachev, Bush and European leaders may be instrumental in this respect. At the December 1988 Washington East-West summit, Gorbachev's offer of unprecedented military reductions coupled with a promised write-off of Third World debts, in the framework of *detente* and a new international economic order could not have been more in keeping with the Cuban analysis and suggests continuing support for the Third World and Cuba. The EEC, meanwhile, is exploring ways of helping Cuba to promote its export products, to in turn help restore import capacity. This could serve as a necessary complement to essentially sound arrangements between Cuba and COMECON, as well as a growing process of Third World or South-South cooperation. It is perhaps not too much to hope that the US might also take its cue from such positive developments.

A change in policy on the part of the US would help to cement Cuba's process of internal democratisation by providing an economic breathing space. The lifting of embargo and the removal of the threat of invasion would necessarily improve economic conditions in the island, reduce alleged dependence on the USSR and do away with the state of siege that has acted as such a powerful constraint to Cuba's development. To do this, however, the US would have to recognise the concept of ideological pluralism and national sovereignty within the Caribbean Basin. At present, such total recognition appears less likely than more partial trading overtures. Yet, were it to happen, it might provide the basis for an economic and political opening that would signal the next phase in the Cuban revolution. As it is, the immediate decisive pressure on Cuba is likely to come from the socialist bloc, for as Castro remarked in December 1988, 'difficulties' can be expected not merely from the island's enemies, but also from its friends. How Cuba responds to such challenges and reacts to fundamental rethinking in the socialist world will very largely determine the course that it takes in the fourth decade of its revolution.

Further Reading

Max Azicri, *Cuba: Politics, Economics and Society*. London, Frances Pinter, 1988

Medea Benjamin, Joseph Collins and Michael Scott, *No Free Lunch: Food and Revolution in Cuba Today*. San Francisco, Food First, 1984

Frei Betto, *Fidel and Religion*. Sydney, Pathfinder, 1986

Peter Bourne, *Castro: A Biography of Fidel Castro*. Basingstoke, Macmillan, 1987

Philip Brenner, *From Confrontation to Negotiation: US Relations with Cuba*. Boulder, Colorado, PACCA/Westview Press, 1988

Claes Brundenius, *Revolutionary Cuba: The Challenge of Economic Growth with Equity*. Boulder, Colorado, Westview Press, 1984

Fidel Castro, *Speeches*. 3 vols, New York, Pathfinder, 1981-5.

Fidel Castro, *The World Crisis: Its Economic and Social Impact on the Underdeveloped Countries*. London, Zed, 1983

Michael Chanan, *The Cuban Image: Cinema and Cultural Politics in Cuba*. London, British Film Institute, 1985.

Jorge Domínguez, *Cuba: Internal and International Affairs*. Beverly Hills, California, Sage, 1982

John Griffiths and Peter Griffiths (eds), *Cuba: The Second Decade*. London, Writers and Readers, 1979

Che Guevara and the Cuban Revolution: Writings and Speeches of Ernesto Che Guevara. Sydney/Havana, Pathfinder/José Martí Publishing House, 1987

Sandor Halebsky and John M. Kirk (eds), *Cuba: Twenty-Five Years of Revolution*, 1959-1984. New York, Praeger, 1985

Barry Lewis and Peter Marshall, *Into Cuba*. London, Zena, 1985

Peter Marshall, *Cuba Libre: Breaking the Chains?* London, Victor Gollancz, 1987

Carmelo Mesa-Lago, *The Economy of Socialist Cuba*. Albuquerque, University of New Mexico Press, 1981

Morris H. Morley, *Imperial State and Revolution: The United States and Cuba*, 1952-1986. Cambridge, Cambridge University Press, 1987

Louis Pérez, *Cuba: Between Reform and Revolution*. New York, Oxford University Press, 1989

Rius, *Cuba for Beginners*. London, Writers and Readers, 1977

Wayne Smith, *The Closest of Enemies: A Personal and Diplomatic History of the Castro Years*. New York, Norton, 1987

Tad Szulc, *Fidel: A Critical Portrait*. New York, William Morrow, 1986

Andrew Zimbalist (ed), *Cuba's Socialist Economy: Toward the 1990s*. Boulder, Colorado, Lynne Rienner, 1988